Contents

HARVEST
Robert Westall

mammoth

First published in Great Britain 1996
by Methuen Children's Books Ltd
Published 1997 by Mammoth
an imprint of Reed International Books Ltd
Michelin House, 81 Fulham Road, London SW3 6RB
and Auckland and Melbourne

The moral rights of the cover illustrator have been asserted.

ISBN 0 7497 2774 8

10 9 8 7 6 5 4 3 2 1

A CIP catalogue record for this title
is available from the British Library

Printed in Great Britain
by Cox & Wyman Ltd, Reading, Berkshire

NOTE TO THE READER

Mau Mau was the name of a secret society formed among the Kikuyu people of Kenya. It was started in the 1940s, and members wanted to drive Europeans out of Kenya. The people who joined Mau Mau had to swear solemn oaths, and there were very severe punishments for anyone who broke a Mau Mau oath. In 1952, members of Mau Mau started a rebellion against the government of Kenya, which was ruled as a British colony. They committed many acts of violence, not just against white people, but against black people who did not support them. The British sent troops to Kenya to put down the Mau Mau rebellion, which went on until 1960. Mau Mau means Get out! Get out!

Chapter One

She travelled by a railway that is long gone. The old North Norfolk line from Peterborough, with its small, hot, black, hissing engines, and the many-doored carriages that already had the sagging weatherbeaten look of the hen-crees and holiday retreats they were soon to become.

Every last detail of that long-lost scene was precious to her. The small, hurrying porters with their open waistcoats and greasy caps; the crates of live white bantams; the dull gleam of silver milk-churns were like hooks that held her sanity in place. The overwhelming smell of soot, the smoke that fragmented through the broken panes of the glass roof into the pale blue, cloud-speckled English sky, even the smuts that settled on the cuffs of her blouse, as she patted her over-tidy hair into place once again, were friends.

'I am in England,' she told herself, like a child uttering a charm against evil. 'I am in England.' And, with a brief spurt of wild hope, extracted a bar of chocolate from a cast-iron vending machine, encrusted with many layers of ancient paint.

The very station names, jolting and burping down from the tannoy, through the dim, shadowed air, were like a blessing and a benediction to her torn mind. Wisbech and South Lynn, Fakenham and Melton Constable seemed to

1

promise, if not peace, at least . . . obscurity. She would settle for obscurity. A green obscurity.

She watched a group hurry past. A stately middle-aged woman, clad most unsuitably for the hot weather in a thick fur coat and black velvet hat. Behind, a porter, forced into an inverted 'V' by the weight of two enormous suitcases. And, in front, a miniature white greyhound, straining at the leash one minute, pausing timidly the next, with paw uplifted, huge eyes bulging in alternate hope and terror.

I am like each of them, she thought. I am encased in layers of deceit. I am carrying a weight I cannot bear. And yet still I strain forward in hope. Hope of *what*? What can *I* possibly hope for?

Wanting peace and quiet, a compartment to herself, she squinted down the platform, working out her tactics. Most of the students were at the far end, where the guard's van would be. Encumbered with bicycles and rucksacks, they were recognising their own kind easily, starting their first flirting rituals. *Which harvest camp are you going to? Which university are you at? What are you reading?* At least they had more verbal ammunition for courtship than those who asked in dance-halls: *isn't it hot?* and *do you come here often? Only in the mating season, harhar.*

I too am a student, she said to herself. I am going to Hickling harvest camp. I am going to read Medicine at London again, after a gap of three years. It was true; but she didn't even believe it herself. And she wasn't ready to join them yet, if she ever would be, in their gentle pushing and poking of each other, their sudden wild giggles, their shouts from one end of the crowd to the other. Her old tweed suit was four years out of date, and far too hot for this weather. But she had left most of her tropical stuff in Africa, and the rest she had given to the jumble as soon as she got home. Nothing was left of Africa, and she sweated out the English summer in old-fashioned wool.

The train pulled in, not more than twenty minutes late. She got a compartment to herself easily. It wasn't hard if you avoided the clustering students. She lifted her heavy suitcase onto the rack, and settled with a travel-magazine called 'Go'. Which didn't have any articles on Africa, because she'd checked.

At first she enjoyed her empty compartment as thoroughly as if it was a newly-rented flat. The seats of large-patterned uncut moquette which, when kicked sharply, sent clouds of golden dust-motes into the air, to linger in the sunbeams from the windows. The framed watercolours of Lincoln Cathedral and Race Week at Cowes. The little green-shaded lights, only two of which worked. The long, low mirrors, frosted with the railway initials, that showed her face, long and dark and sallow with dead sunburn. But her eyes flicked away from looking into her mirror-eyes, frightened of what they might see. Her eyes were too big these days, too staring. Too much the eyes of a murderess. She had begun to understand recently why King Oedipus had blinded himself.

At that, all her tiny pleasures fled. Once the whistling porter had walked the length of the train, slamming the doors, she would be alone, for there were no corridors on these trains. Alone with herself, all the way to Wisbech. It threw her into a panic. She considered hauling down the huge suitcase and changing carriages, hurling herself . . . not in among the students but into some compartment where there might be an old man, or a solid housewife with her basket full of cheerful and irrelevant groceries. But it was too late; the guard's whistle was blowing. The door-slamming porter swept past her, with his crescendo of

3

bangs, and dwindled off towards the engine. The carriage thrummed into some obscure life above her head. The train gave a couple of sharp jerks, one in each direction. She was trapped. With no one to look at, no living person who might smile, speak, scratch or read a book with mysterious, satisfied grunts. No anchor in the present time; no policeman to control her treacherous mind and stop her from weeping or screaming or clawing at her own face to distract the inner pain.

Then her carriage door was snatched open, just as the train started to move. A large young man with fair hair threw a huge rucksack wildly in. One of its straps caught her stockinged leg with a sharp sting. With a heave, he hauled himself in after it, and leaned out again to grab the swinging door. A porter shouted angrily, and the young man waved back – a large gesture that held apology, and at the same time, glee. Then he heaved his rucksack up on the rack, catching her leg again, said, 'Sorry about this!' and dropped into the seat opposite. He had a grin that expected instant forgiveness of all his sins, that quite swept her off her feet, so that she smiled in return. He was undoubtedly a student. No mere farm labourer would dare to dress so weirdly. Winter corduroy trousers with summer sandals, an open-necked check shirt and a sleeveless leather jerkin from the Army and Navy Stores.

At the same time, she saw him assess that she was *not* a student. A slight tinge of disappointment clouded his face as he came to the conclusion that she was bourgeois, a secretary or something, and definitely *not* someone to chat up. It made her feel unbearably old, at the age of twenty-four. It made her feel, once again, that her life was over.

She put him down as nineteen or twenty. He thought he could get away with shaving only once every two or three days. The blond fluff on his chin was endearing, like the fluff on a duckling.

He leapt to his feet again, groped in the side pocket of the rucksack, so that a blue towel fell out, decided he was groping in the wrong pocket, heaved the rucksack over, took a crumpled *Manchester Guardian* from the other side pocket, and buried himself in it.

He was reading the sport on the back page. The front page headline said:

ARMY CLAIM SOME SUCCESS
AGAINST THE MAU MAU

She shuddered as the carriage went cold and dark around her; as she bit her lip till she drew blood, the usual slight taste of salt. As her hands dug into the stiff moquette of the seats like a pair of claws.

But he was reading, and he did not notice.

She tried to lose herself in the passing back gardens. The train went so slowly, as it always had done, that she seemed to have time to study every garden in detail. Show me a garden and you show me a family. The pride of a pensioner in a newly-mown lawn, a newly-painted garden seat with its folded newspaper and half-drunk mug of coffee. The clutter of a young family, with a row of washing diminishing in size, and a lawn littered with bits of brightly-coloured toys. The splendour of a show-winning gardener, with fat rows of weedless cabbages and leeks, and the bright red and green glitter of runner-beans. The garden full of weeds that meant adultery or illness or death.

'Excuse me, you haven't got a match, have you?'

'Yes, I have, actually. Well, a lighter, anyway.' Why should she have to apologize for having a lighter? She looked up from her handbag to find him waving a blue packet of Gauloises in her face.

'Would you like one?'

'I haven't had a Gauloise for years!'

'I've just been to France. They're very cheap over there. They're awful things. The paper's dipped in saltpetre to make it burn – see those little sparks it gives off – but it still drops off in great charred lumps.'

'I like the smell of them.'

Having lit up, he dug in the pocket of his jerkin, produced a dog-eared copy of Kafka's *The Trial* and immersed himself in it, his cheek against the glass of the window and his neck at such an unnatural angle that it would have been agony to anyone who was not twenty years old. He was so utterly relaxed, like a young dog.

Oh why do you fill your mind with Kafka's darkness, she wondered, when you are so young and happy? Then she smiled, bitterly, remembering. Remembering herself being so young and happy that Kafka was a dark, exciting sauce.

But he did not settle to the book long. Her acceptance of a Gauloise had obviously bothered him; made it impossible to write her off as a secretary or something. He kept on throwing her surreptitious glances.

'Have you been to France?'

'Several times. When I was a student.'

'Oh.' He was greatly impressed. 'What do you do now?'

'Still a student.' She laughed, awkwardly. 'Third year medic at King's, London. I gave it up for a while. I went . . . abroad.'

'Oh,' he said. 'You didn't look like a student.' He looked at her sober suit; her big suitcase.

'Actually, I'm going to a student harvest camp. At Hickling.'

He looked at her suit and case again, now distinctly worried.

'It's a bit rough at Hickling, you know. Just Army bell-tents and chemical loos and a big green hut we eat in.'

A bit rough . . . she remembered for an instant the endless dry plain of Africa, the baked, rutted road to the mission, the sores on the children's legs, the stink of the villages. Then dragged her mind back to the railway compartment, with the endless green and soft vegetable smells of England, flowing in through the windows. 'I'm quite used to roughing it. I'm not made of barley-sugar. I don't melt in the rain.'

'I didn't mean you looked soft . . .' He studied her, as if searching for a word. Somehow she couldn't mind his scrutiny. It was the open wondering scrutiny of a child, still.

He could not find the word he wanted; or else he didn't want to utter it. Instead, he said, 'Hickling's not bad. You have to watch out for the midges and horseflies. The horseflies are bastards, but there's a second between them landing and them putting their jaws into you. You just have time to squash them, if you're quick. Otherwise you come up in a lump like . . .' He sounded protective. What he had seen in her had made him *protective*. She had come home with the mark of Cain, and he was treating her like the Prodigal Son. It made her feel alive inside just for a second. It gave her an absurd desire to cry. But he seemed to have noticed nothing. His eyes were on the painting of Lincoln Cathedral, as he said:

'Potato picking's the worst. Breaks your back. Met an old boy last summer who said it didn't use to be so bad. In the old days, the men got tired but the horse got tired as

7

well, so it went slower with the cart. Now they have tractors, and tractors never get tired . . .'

'Yes,' she said. 'I can see that.' She listened to her own
voice carefully, but it seemed steady enough.

'It's good in the evenings and at weekends. We all go
down to the Pleasure Boat for a drink. Have a sing-song.
Or we go sailing. You can hire a dinghy for a quid. Can you
sail?'

'No.'

'I'll teach you, if you like.'

'Thank you very much.' The wonderful thing, she
thought, was that there was so little overtone in his voice.
No pity, no horror, no condemnation. Not even an attempt
to pick her up. Only a tone as if she was an aunt, to be
taken care of. It made her feel very old indeed. But nice.
She felt an absurd desire to tease him; she could not remember when she had last teased anybody.

'How old do you think I am, then?'

A look of horror crossed his face, at being asked to do
such a thing. 'My mother says you should never ask a lady
her age.'

'This time the lady's asking you.'

'Dunno,' he said at last. 'You look . . . grown up. The lot
at the camp are just an overgrown bunch of kids.'

'I'm only twenty-four.'

The look on his face crushed her. She must look much
much older than twenty-four. Then he dived back into his
book, and she was sorry. It was as if she'd made friends with
a stray dog, then frightened it away again.

They both hid behind their reading; but such a barrier was
no longer enough. The compartment was too small and too
hot, and the trackside greenery came in too close, brushing

8

against the carriage window in places with a soft deafening rustling; as if the railway was losing the fight with a green jungle, and they might be on the last train to get through. Every breath of air, when the engine occasionally picked up speed, was welcomed by them both with the same deep grateful sighs. They sweated together, moved their bodies the same way to try to cool them. They became as familiar with each other's moves and sighings as a married couple in bed . . . her mind jammed down a shutter on that one. She refused to think about married couples in beds. She took her jacket off, and loosened the top button on her blouse, having made sure he wasn't watching. He flung off his jerkin along the seat so that it half fell to the dirty floor, and she had to fight an impulse to tidy it. He undid three buttons of his shirt, one after another, with even shyer wary looks at her. Then he exploded the tension into bathos, by trying to fan air with his book down the gap he had made. He was what he said all the others were; an overgrown kid. The hair on his chest was as soft and downy as the hair on his chin.

He said one more thing. He stuck his head on one side in a profound owlish way and said, 'I get the illusion on this train that it's going on for ever. That time stands still. That we'll never get to Wisbech or South Lynn or anywhere . . .'

She laughed, and said, 'Isn't that the charm of it?'

He frowned. 'Not really. I want to get somewhere. I've lived more than a quarter of my life, and I haven't done anything yet but pass exams. I mean, exams aren't *real*, are they? You can't make a living passing exams.'

But she didn't really realise how close they'd become till Wisbech. There, an old countryman got into their compartment, wearing a long, dirty raincoat. The boy moved his jerkin and paper with a very ill grace. The old man felt an *intruder*; a destroyer of some deep content, some green primal Eden. Besides, he smelt; a rancid, feral smell. And his little mean blue eyes were everywhere. As if he was trying to get a reaction out of them . . .

Then she noticed movements under the dirty raincoat . . . she held her breath and nearly screamed at him. Until a tiny, pale ferret pushed its head out of one of the raincoat pockets, and surveyed the carriage with bright quick red eyes. There was another ferret in the other pocket, too. The old man took advantage of the surprise they caused to go into a long lecture on the ways of ferrets, which they had to listen to, whether they liked it or not.

All the time, she told herself to have Christian charity; that he was just a lonely old man; and quite interesting, really, on the habits of ferrets; and the beasts were quite beautiful in their quick feral way; and they too were Creatures of God. . . .

He got off at South Lynn, and they both heaved a deep sigh of relief, caught each other at it, and laughed.

Then the boy said, in impersonation, 'When 'ee do put the old ferret down the 'ole . . .' and they both collapsed helplessly.

It was to be a running joke between them, right to the end.

On they dawdled, into the green of the land, and slowly it got cooler, and the air flowing through the window might have held a hint of the sea. Frequently, the train stopped at nowhere, for no fathomable reason. Between Fakenham and Melton Constable the train not only stopped at nowhere, but she saw the driver and the fireman descend the embankment, and go into the back door of a trackside cottage.

'Gone for their tea,' said the boy. 'They usually do that here. Now we're stuck for twenty minutes, at least. All right for some.'

'Could you give me a hand down with my case? I've got a small flask of tea and some sandwiches.'

When he had put the case back, he dug into the pockets of his rucksack, and produced a very squashed half-loaf of brown bread and a sticky half-packet of dates. He saw her looking at them, and said, embarrassed, 'They seemed sensible when I bought them. Healthy. Didn't need any knives or forks or messing . . .'

She gave a helpless snort of laughter, amazing herself again. Then said, 'Would you like some of mine? I've made far too many.'

She had a sandwich-tin full of tiny white triangles of cucumber and tomato sandwiches, with their crusts cut off. They seemed almost as ridiculously feminine as his had seemed masculine. Especially when he ate them in large numbers. As her father would've said, it was like feeding an elephant strawberries.

'Since we're sharing a meal, perhaps we ought to know each other's names?'

'Brian Trench,' he said abruptly, his mouth comically full of sandwich.

'Philippa Moran.'

He shook hands very formally. After that, he talked a lot. A weird and wonderful mixture. He tried Existentialism, but had the grace to sense he was boring her. He was much more interesting on all his friends and relations. There was an everyday happiness that just bubbled out of him. And yet . . . he seemed a happy boy in search of unhappiness.

11

Avid for some great tragic deeper meaning to life. A happy pig desperate to become an unhappy philosopher.

Of course, having been told so much of somebody else's life, she was overwhelmingly tempted to tell him something of her own. She stuck rigidly to the time before she left school. Before she had even clapped eyes on Max.

He loved her pictures of Daddy the absent-minded vicar. Knocking the water-carafe off the pulpit with an extra-sweeping gesture in the middle of a sermon. Coming down and picking up the broken glass on his hands and knees, while continuing to drone on about the Trinity. . . . The desperate wrangles in the parochial church council about the house-martins that nested in the Sunday School roof and threatened to drop droppings on the Bishop when he came. . . . She found she could make him laugh, and his laugh was so young and refreshing she wanted to make him laugh more and more.

And yet there came the horrible moment when the laughter finally died, and they were left looking at each other too intimately, and she found his eyes trying to probe into her very soul.

She had an awful conviction that he sensed the darkness in her, and that was what he really wanted.

They were saved by a signal box that said 'North Walsham'.

'Time to go,' he said, getting to his feet. 'If I take your case, can you get my bike from the guard's van?'

The next second, the train was jerking and squealing to a halt.

Chapter Two

There was a canvas-covered lorry waiting for them in the station yard, marked North Norfolk Fruit Farms. All the students gathered at the back. Brian's arrival was hailed with shouts and hand-shaking and back-slapping and reminiscences of last year, and a lot of last year's in-jokes which the newcomers, standing open-mouthed on the fringes, obviously didn't understand. It was also obvious Brian was popular; it gave her a sudden absurd twinge of jealousy, and she felt unutterably and ridiculously lonely. Had she really built up a dream of having him all to herself?

One young giant in particular was doing a lot of shouting and joking and back-slapping. He left nobody in any doubt he was Irish, even perhaps a member of the IRA, but his name seemed to be Mick Schneider, which was an odd name for an Irishman. He had a heavy-boned Germanic face, worthy of the Waffen SS, and a huge pair of goggling spectacles. That was all they needed, a German stage-Irishman. She took an instant dislike to him. Brian turned a lot noisier in his company, as if he was in competition to make the most noise, and they were putting a lot of the newcomers off.

At that point, she felt a slight tug at her sleeve. A woman was standing there, a couple of years older than herself and every inch the schoolmistress.

'Hello,' said the woman, ruefully. 'Nice to see another adult in this bedlam. I knew the young could be a bit much, but didn't know they could be as bad as this. I came for a bit of country life and university conversation, but *really*.' She held out her hand. 'My name's Doreen Broderick. You can call me Brod. Are you sharing a tent with anyone?'

The driver of the van shouted in a surly voice, 'Are we going to stay here all day?' and Brian got things moving with an energy only equalled by Mick Schneider, heaving bikes aboard, then rucksacks and suitcases, then girls. There was much squealing and shrieking and showing of leg as the girls were pushed up over the tailgate.

'Like a damned Viking raid,' hissed Brod acidly. 'Without the pillaging. Girls do make themselves so *cheap*.'

Philippa wished to God she'd keep her voice down and the disapproval off her face. Some of the students were summing her up already; a barrier was growing, a silence, around the pair of them. Any minute, they could end up in a ghetto of two that would last the whole length of the camp.

'They're not hauling me up like a sack of rubbish,' said Brod. 'Or getting a look at *my* suspenders . . .'

Perhaps Brian heard her. He came across and said, 'I've arranged for you two to ride in the cab with the driver.' He did not smile; already his face was the face of a stranger. He led them round to the cab, and held the door open for them politely. Philippa could have wept. Not that she wanted to show off her suspenders to the young man exactly . . . but she could see a month of Brod, Brod, Brod, looming ahead.

At the far end of the journey, there was a disorganised older

14

student with a beard and a clipboard, who said he was called Terry and that he was the Camp Organiser. His organisation seemed to consist of trying to tick people off on his list (usually the wrong people, who objected) and pointing the way up a narrow cinder-track between high hawthorn hedges. 'Straight on. Women to the right of the Shed, men to the left. You can choose your own tents.'

Brian vanished, carrying the rucksacks of half a dozen girls who were plucking at his shoulders and shrieking in his ears, all at once. Philippa and Brod were left with their huge suitcases.

'For us,' said Brod, 'the age of chivalry is dead. How I hate these young pups.' They struggled up the cinder-track, past a huge hut with a verandah, painted bright green. A lot of thin brown army mattresses were still piled against its walls, and there was a litter of enamel bowls and Elsans lying on their sides.

'The Shed, obviously,' said Brod. 'The very centre of our civilisation. I hope you brought your own lavatory paper. I can foresee many a trip into the trackless woods . . . .'

They found their tent easily enough. It was the only one left empty. At the far end of the line from the Shed; and from the canvas tent marked 'Ablutions'; and the canvas screen marked with a cock-eyed sign saying 'Ladies'. There was a dense bed of nettles outside the tent, some of which had managed to get inside too, where they poked up evilly between the tent walls and the wooden duckboards on the floor, and lurked beneath the army beds. There were striped pillows but no pillowcases; brown blankets and only one huge sheet each. The only other items were an oily leaking hurricane lamp hung from a nail on the tent-pole, and a list of the tent's contents, which said that they would be responsible for any losses. The place was as hot as an oven, and smelt of paraffin, nettles and cow-dung.

'Home, sweet homicide,' said Brod. 'About par for the course.'

'You've been to harvest camps before, then?'

'Every year since I left college. And every year it gets worse.'

'So why do you come?'

'*You* try getting to Rome on what boarding-school teachers get paid. The life of genteel poverty. Two per cent genteel and ninety-eight per cent poverty.' Brod sat on her bed heavily (she'd chosen the one nearest the door and the light and the fresh air). Philippa looked at her. She must have been twenty-six or seven; not unattractive. Long smooth dark hair, large dark eyes, a nice figure and plump but shapely legs. But there were frown-marks on her smooth high forehead, and the corners of her mouth turned down sourly. A pretty rose with the worm already in it, as William Blake might have said.

'I'm going to deal with these nettles,' said Philippa. She just had to get outside.

'You'll get no help from that chinless wonder with the beard,' Brod called after her. 'I know the type. They're usually trainee vicars. The NUS thinks they give the camp an aura of respectability . . .'

It didn't improve Philippa's temper to walk down the row of tents. Every one seemed to be full of lively femininity, with delighted shrieks, the hanging up of clothes on hangers from tent-poles, and the warm mutter of shared intimacy. Girls were already passing from tent to tent, half-naked. Only she was outside. With Brod.

At the Shed, Terry was still asking newcomers their names and addresses, and crossing out and scribbling on

ne of themselves. Funny. Brod made yawning gulfs,
rian built bridges over them.

ght,' said Brian, throwing his sodden tea-towel over
t of string stretched across the window. 'The pub.'

y walked down the cinder-track in the early dusk,
her girls discussing the work-prospects for Monday
g.

ll get raspberries,' said Jane, the fat one. 'Men aren't
od at berries; the farmers won't have them. Too
Squash the fruit.'

n,' said Brian. 'I'm great at blackcurrants. Lie on
k and pull 'em down in great bunches. Four pun-
y, and that's a quid.'

punnets of blackcurrant jam,' said the thin one,
m full of stalks. He squashes them so badly we
over them up with ours, or the farmer wouldn't
. . .'

sk, pleasantly tired legs, cool breeze rustling the
in the field beside them; far above, the swifts
nd screaming faint as stars. When had she last
peace . . .?

it was there before her eyes again. The wind,
ry as an open oven, blowing up the dried soil
ion yard into little whirling dust-devils. The
ssed-down limbs that would never move again.
h split and oozed and *exploded*. The expression
caricature smeared on dead clay by a sculptor
t or feeling. The first faint whiff, from the
ls, of decay. . . .

Philippa?' She heard Brian's anxious call, and
stopped dead in her tracks, and the others
back from ten yards ahead. And the vision

20

his clipboard. But some of the other men were carrying
mattresses and bowls and filled Elsans in a purposeful way.
Brian was right in the thick of it, doing about a dozen
things at once, stripped to the waist. His white back was
already showing ominous pink signs of sunburn, but he
seemed blissfully happy.

'Nettles? Right!' he said. 'Be with you in a jiffy. Terry,
where's the bloody billhook?' Terry waved his long white
hands ineffectually towards the Shed. Brian rummaged
inside, heaving trestle tables in all directions, and located
it. They walked back together, the girls from every tent
shouting rude remarks about Brian's semi-nudity which he
acknowledged with a lordly wave of hand and billhook.
Philippa fell a few paces behind fearing decapitation. He
turned, looking for her, and said, 'I love the *start* of things.
And the *end* of things. It's the middle that gets a bit
boring.'

In the tent, he said how-do to Brod, knelt down, and
began massacring the nettles by the tent-wall like Genghis
Khan.

Brod just sat watching him, her skirt pulled up to cool
her plump thighs, her blouse unbuttoned one button too
many. For a woman who looked to the classical beauties of
Rome, she had a strange air of defeat and sensuality that
disturbed Philippa in the presence of a young man. She
looked at Brian, but he was blissfully unaware, now hacking at the nettles under the empty bed. Philippa got a
feeling that Brian was blind to what he didn't want to see.

'Right!' said Brian, finally getting up from hacking nettles to within an inch of Brod's legs. 'That's done for them
for the moment. If you want to borrow the billhook again,
just ask *me*.'

He walked away to renewed banter from the other tents.

17

'Young *lout*,' said Brod viciously. 'He might have cleared them up for us. Just look at the mess he's made!'

The dinner, served on enamel plates, was solid but uninspired. Thick slices of melting corned beef, boiled potatoes on the point of floury disintegration, baked beans. Custard and rags of prunes to follow. Brod turned up her nose but ate every scrap. They were at one end of a long table, but the rest of the people at the table ignored them, though they conducted shouted conversations with friends several tables away. A perceptible gap opened on the two long benches. Only a foot, but it might have been a mile, between the young and those condemned as middle-aged.

After the meal, Terry, clipboard still in one hand, banged for silence with the other, using a dirty metal plate that spread drops of custard all over the table-top. He was already being referred to as the Clipboard King.

'First, washing-up,' he said, diffidently staring at the wreckage of the meal. 'We'll have a rota out by tomorrow, but can I have volunteers for tonight?'

There was a stony silence. One of the men muttered, 'Waste of good drinking time,' and got a laugh.

Finally Brian, who was sitting beside Terry said; 'Oh come on, you rotten lot. Who'll give me a hand?' He looked touchingly indignant, and about twelve years old.

'I will,' said Philippa loudly. Every face turned to stare at her. Several of the female faces looked quite hostile. Somebody muttered, 'Teacher's pet.' Then several of the girls volunteered together; the Brian-effect was working again.

'Right,' said Terry, relief in his voice. 'Now to matters of administration . . .'

There were loud groans all round. After half an hour

of Terry's interminable mumbling abou
packed lunches, and transport, Philippa

'*Finally*,' said Terry, to a ribald cheer
Camp Chairman and Committee.
responsible . . .'

'Brian,' shouted somebody. 'He's th
'Seconded,' shouted somebody else
all the slog . . .'

'Mick Schneider,' shouted someb
an ugly laugh.

Philippa saw the looks that pa
Mick, when nobody else was watch
other's backs they might. But
between them; no love at all.

Brian won the vote by thirty-
But she had a nasty feeling th

It shouldn't have been much f
kitchen, with not a trace of a
wide-open window and door
the huge stove. But the jol
clowning; Brian walking ar
on the end of his snub nose
plates at once, Brian claw
sides of the huge dixie wit
around with raised claw
Hickling. Brian seemed
girls laugh. They seeme
nal property; there was
jealousy. They ended up

He had treated Phil
but he called her Phil
other girls were calli

like
and
'R
the b
The
the ot
mornir
'We
any go
clumsy.
'Go
your bac
nets a da
'Four
Sally. 'Ja
have to c
take them
Blue du
long oats
wheeling a
known suc
And the
harsh and
of the miss
carelessly to
The way fles
of the face, a
without taler
exposed bowe
'You OK,
found she had
were looking
was gone. . . .

18

'I'm just tired,' she called. 'Sorry.' And ran gratefully to catch them up.

'What you need is a drink,' said Brian.

The Pleasure Boat was a very old pub, a long low place, whitewashed and thatched, with a jetty sticking out into Hickling Broad. There were seven or eight big lush cabin-cruisers moored, and men and women, immaculate in white flannels with sweaters slung round their necks, coming ashore, bronzed and relaxed, for an evening's fun. From inside the pub came the sound of voices raised in song. The other students were already in session.

I give you ten-oh
   Green grow the rushes oh!
What are your ten-oh . . .

Inside the students stood in two factions. The big group of singers, who greeted Brian with jubilant yells and quite savage punches. And five or six round Mick Schneider at the far end of the bar, propping up the wall with superior sneers on their faces. The people off the cabin-cruisers sat around with amused tolerant looks on their faces, as if they regarded singing students as a treat, a bit of the local colour. Nostalgia for student days that some of them had probably never had.

'A pint for Brian,' yelled somebody.

'Which he will once again fail to drink without stopping,' called Mick Schneider nastily.

'You're on, Mick,' said Brian. 'What you betting?'

'Five bob.'

'Right!' Brian surveyed the pint in his hand, took a deep breath, raised the glass, threw back his head.

'One,' counted the assembled mob, as his Adam's apple heaved. 'Two, three, four, five . . . six . . . seven . . . eight.'

Philippa found that her hands were clenched, that she was willing Brian on. *Anything* to take that smirk off Schneider's face.

'Nine . . . ten!'

Brian banged down the pint-pot, empty, and surveyed the foam draining back down the sides with a dreamy eye.

'That's five bob you owe me come pay-day, Schneider.'

Then the dreamy look turned to one of alarm. With a desperate gulp, he ran out of the bar and past the window towards the Broad, amidst a storm of cheering and booing. Far off, Philippa heard the sound of splashing and retching.

'That lets me off,' said Schneider. 'He owes me five bob now.'

'Go on,' said somebody. 'He bet you he could *drink* it. He never said *digest* it.'

'You bloody philosophy students . . .'

Brian had reappeared, looking distinctly pale.

'You all right?' asked Philippa, anxiously.

'Fine. There is an art in throwing up, like the old Romans used at banquets. A noble art. Straight out, can't let it hit the back of your teeth, or your mouth tastes foul all night . . . the fishes queue at this end of the Broad in the evenings to get a chance to get pissed for nothing . . . that's still five bob you owe me, Schneider. Let's have another song . . .'

The landlord behind the bar smiled with professional goodwill; the tourists were really enjoying the show as the new song belted out across the quiet fish-plopping Broad.

Oh, Sir Jasper do not touch me
   Oh, Sir Jasper do not touch me
Oh, Sir Jasper do not touch me

As she slipped between the lily-white sheets with nothing on at all.

And Philippa kept having ten-second flashes of a dead face.

Chapter Three

On Monday morning, it turned out to be blackcurrants. The farmer had sent a tractor and trailer for them. They strolled out into the sunshine after breakfast, still dopey from the pub the previous night, burping on a full load of bacon, egg and fried bread, feeling like anything but work.

They piled aboard, grumbling about the trailer, which had a work-polished steel load-bed, liberally streaked with what looked like dried manure. Trailers were the worst; you couldn't avoid the filth and the bumping by standing up, like you could with a lorry.

Most of the girls were in very short shorts and halter tops. Philippa, with the wisdom of East Africa, thought they'd be sorry by the end of the day. Sunburnt back and thighs were no joke. She herself was wearing an old long-sleeved shirt, slacks and shoes. Blackcurrants had prickly twigs. But she still felt an ancient, joyless frump.

Even Brian was silent, as they bumped over the grass-grown ruts of the blackcurrant fields, the steel load-bed banging away nastily at the bottom of their spines, so they put down their lunch-boxes and sat on their clenched fists.

'First ten rows,' said the farmer. 'And I'll not pay for squashed ones. Bring every punnet back to the weighing-machine as you finish it.' He was a burly, withdrawn man, in a three-piece suit and cap, carrying a stick, and Philippa thought he classed students as something between ailing pigs and the village women, certainly not a patch on the village women. Suddenly, she felt mutinous.

But it was a bliss to get among the blackcurrants, the deep cool shade spattered with sunlight, the sharp, sweet smell as she felt for the first invisible bunch under the little intricate leaves, enclosed it with gentle fingers, like a lover, and pulled downwards.

'Don't eat any,' said someone behind her. 'He checks your mouth every time you weigh-in.'

Yet it was a green Eden you could get lost in, the sun in small patches on your back, the little clusters of berries so perfect, with their finger-smudged bloom of blue-grey . . .

'That you, Philippa?' asked Brod's voice from the far side of the bush. 'We might as well work as a pair. I'll pick what you miss.'

Peace fled. Brod's voice never stopped, and seldom stopped criticizing.

'The way those young girls dress, showing everything they've got. God knows what they're up to with the lads. It's more like a brothel than a farm. I swear two of them are on the game. I heard them talking . . .' She seemed to have no idea of how her voice carried, of how close, among the rustling rows, the other students were.

At other times she turned on her school.

'Why is it that my one free period on a Monday always coincides with the Head's RK lesson with the fifth form? She always gets a phone-call in the middle of it, and is away for the rest of the lesson, and guess who has to fill in for her . . .

'The Deputy Head is supposed to be a mathematician

and she can't even cut the cake into twelve equal portions at the end-of-term party.'

The carefree chatter from down the rows turned into a low rumbling song, that grew in volume and sarcasm.

'Why was she born so beautiful, why was she born at all . . .'

Philippa shut her eyes because she couldn't shut her ears. She wondered if death was preferable to this.

By lunchtime, she had picked four punnets, which was a quid already. She had picked fast and hard, to blot out the sound of that voice. She had picked faster and harder to try to leave the voice behind altogether. To be met with a wail.

'Don't go so *fast*, Philippa. You're *leaving* half of them. It's not fair on the farmer . . .'

She wasn't. She'd made sure she picked her side of the bushes clean. It was Brod who was leaving half of them, on *her* side, in her desperation to keep up. Otherwise, why had she only weighed-in three punnets to Philippa's four?

God, I'm starting to think like her, now, thought Philippa.

She walked off to the barn, where they could have lunch in the shade, on bales of straw.

'Wait for *me*, Philippa, what's the rush?' Under the weight of the heat of the day, Brod's immaculate Oxford English was starting to break down into something more like cockney.

Philippa kept on walking, with a sudden surge of vicious cruelty. As she came into the dark of the barn, and her eyes adjusted, she saw a bale of straw with a man student sitting on each end, and dropped down in the narrow space between them. They moved their backs to make room for her, without a word, wriggling their objections. But at least there, Brod could not get at her.

Except that Brod looked round desperately and came over and sat in the dirt at her feet.

'You'd think gentlemen would give up their seat to a *lady*,' she said, in a very loud voice.

One of the two men students got up and stalked off without a word . . .

After lunch, as they were getting up with groans and aching backs, to go back to work, the farmer came in.

'I need two for lifting potatoes . . .'

There was stony silence. Leave the shade of the blackcurrants for an open field? You could take a rest among the bushes when it got too hot. But in the potato-field, the tractor never stopped . . .

'Look,' said the farmer, angrily. 'I don't have to employ you lot at all . . .'

'OK,' said Brian wearily. 'I'll do it.'

'And so will I,' said Philippa. Even a crippled back was preferable to Brod.

They walked off to the tractor and trailer together. She heard a mutter among the girls.

'She must *really* fancy him. . . .'

'Cradle-snatching. . . .'

'Christ,' said Brian, taking a quick look at his watch, swiping the brown dust off its face with a sweaty hand. 'Still an hour to go. I'd like to *smash* that bloody machine.'

The tractor swept past them again, with a black stink of half-burnt paraffin, dragging the sun-glinting blade behind that exposed a fresh band of damp earth, and another endless straggling galaxy of golden potatoes.

They bent their aching backs again, side by side, dragging the half-filled sacks behind them. Brian was doing the lion's share of the picking, still. In the beginning, she had fought back, poaching on his side, trying to keep the score even. Now she knew she couldn't cope without his misplaced gallantry.

'This is no job for a woman,' he raged.

'The village women do it!'

'Most of them are built like navvies . . .'

'Tripe.' In spite of his gallantry, she was starting to lose her temper with him. An aching back could turn you into a devil.

'What did you volunteer for? *Our* women *never* do it!'

'What's this "our" women? I thought you were a Socialist?'

'Doctors need sensitive hands, to operate on people. You'll end up with callouses like me Dad. Why *did* you volunteer, anyway?'

'To get away from Brod. She does nothing but bitch, bitch, bitch.'

'Oh, *that*. She always starts off like that. Till she gets what she's looking for. She's better after that.'

'What do you mean – what she's looking for?'

'Nothing.' He concentrated on picking up potatoes.

'I insist you tell me what you meant!'

'Leave it.' He sounded angry, embarrassed, ashamed. She knew it was best if she left it. But she was angry, hot, sweaty and fed up that she couldn't leave him alone. She wanted to punch the curve of his bending backside.

'I *insist* that you tell me.'

He stood upright, his hands going straight up to ease his back. 'All right, since you *insist*. She comes to these camps looking for a *man*. Anything in trousers that will have her.

Then she shuts up. It's the same every year.' He glared at her, ashamed and defiant, like a child.

'I suppose you think I've come for the same reason?' Stupid tears started in her eyes.

He suddenly looked very solemn, as if he had just entered a church.

'No,' he said slowly. 'I don't think that. You're a *lady*.'

'Why do you think I've come, then?' She wondered why it should be so important to her, his opinion.

'I think you were happy here once, and you've come back to look for it again.' Then he turned away and began picking up more potatoes. Silently she followed his silent back, picking in her turn. So that was what he thought, the young pup! Nostalgia for a lost harvest camp affair, long ago. The incurable young romantic! If he only knew! Her mind swept back to that dusty mission yard again, the dead face. . . .

But the tractor roared past again, and Brian gave a despairing yell. 'Come *on*. We haven't finished *this* row yet!'

Then, twenty yards ahead, the tractor gave a tremendous smoky snort, and simply stopped, leaning over in a furrow. The farmer came running along the line, shouting wildly. The tractor-driver yelled back at him. Then the farmer snatched a jerrycan off the back of the tractor and waved it in the driver's face.

'Glory be,' said Brian. 'I think they've run out of fuel. And it'll take him twenty minutes to go for more. And he's got to pay us by the hour, and it's nearly half-past four.' He grabbed her and waltzed her around through the furrows, so that they fell over and sat down with a soft soily bump.

They grinned at each other, as if they'd won a famous victory.

29

'We're all going swimming tonight,' said Brian. 'At Sea Palling. You coming?'

She thought there was nothing she'd rather have in all the world than a swim in the sea.

They gathered at the Shed after tea, about twenty of them, half boys and half girls; everyone carrying a towel and costume. Philippa stood on the edge, feeling rather shy and out of it, and wondering how they were going to get there. The boys all seemed to have bikes, but none of the girls had. There must be a lorry coming for them, or at least a tractor and trailer. Thank God she had something to cushion her bottom against the bumps.

But nothing had shown up when Mick Schneider said, with a stare at her, 'We all here, lass? Mount up!'

And in a second, every boy was astride his bike, and every one had a girl with him. Some girls perched on the bikes' carriers, trailing their long bare graceful legs and letting their toes touch the ground on each side. Some girls sat on the saddles, while the boy stood on his pedals. Some girls sat on the cross-bars on their towels, between the boys' pedalling wide-splayed knees. But in a second, they were moving off down the road, as smooth, slow and graceful as a flock of swimming swans.

And she was left alone. Standing like a fool with her towel and costume in her hand. She blushed with a deep embarrassment, though there was no one to notice. She turned away blindly, before anyone could come by and notice her misery. And as she turned, she came face to face with Brian, wheeling his bike. And with a girl, and they were laughing together.

Brian's eyes went to her towel and costume, and his face filled with dismay and distress.

30

'Have the rotten sods gone off and left you? I was sure somebody would give you a lift . . .'

'Well, they *haven't*. Would you mind getting out of the way?' Her voice was more cutting than she meant it to be. She was just desperate to run away and hide. Anywhere.

'Look,' said Brian. 'We can't have *this*.'

'I don't want your *charity*!'

'Look, Sylvia here's got a bike of her own. Haven't you, Sylvia?'

'I suppose so,' said Sylvia.

'Look, Sylv, be a *sport*. Then we can all have a swim.'

'I don't think I'll bother,' said Sylv, and turned away and walked off between the tents with a stiff back.

'Hell, that's torn it,' said Brian. He sounded surprised and hurt. 'She had no need to take it like that. I hardly know her . . .'

She could have wept for his naivety. She said, 'Whatever career you go in for, Brian, don't make it the Diplomatic Corps.'

'But I didn't mean to hurt anybody's feelings . . .'

'That's what Hitler said in 1939 . . .'

He laughed. He laughed and laughed and laughed.

'You're quite a *wit*, Philippa!'

'Don't be so bloody patronising. Or I might walk out on you too. It isn't really your night, is it?'

'I can't open my big mouth without putting my foot in it.'

He looked so crestfallen, she couldn't help forgiving him. Then he said very humbly,

'D'you want a lift, then?'

'Two on one bike's illegal.'

'Not a village bobby within miles.'

'What about the hills?'

'No hills round here.'

'It looks . . . impossible.'

'Try it. On the cross-bar. Towel as a cushion.'

Gingerly, she sat on, resting her hands on the middle of the handlebars. His large bare arms, with their tiny gold hairs, enclosed her. He gave a heave and a grunt and they were miraculously moving. His large thighs brushed her knees on one side and her bottom on the other. They turned out of the cinder lane, and swept on towards the distant sea.

'See, it works!' He said it gleefully, like a kid, a happy show-off kid. With his mouth just above the hair on top of her head, which stirred in the soft warm wind of their passage. She watched rows of poplar-trees and telegraph poles slip by, as if in a dream. For the first time since she'd married Max, she felt utterly, childishly *safe*. Daddy's little girl again, cossetted, indulged, approved of.

Above her head, totally unaware of her bliss, Brian prattled on.

'I'm sorry about them leaving you like that. The trouble is, they've all paired off by this time. Nothing serious, of course. But it's nice to have somebody steady to knock around with, while the camp lasts. Then they go home, swearing eternal friendship, and never even write to each other till the next year. It's a funny place, harvest camp . . .'

And later.

'That's the ruined mill we have midnight picnics in sometimes. Way off beyond those trees there. Very spooky. They do say it's haunted, though we've never seen anything yet . . .'

But his voice was no more important than the chirr of his freewheel, or the spat of gravel beneath his tyres. She just borrowed the feel of his arms and his legs, and his breathing, and the sweet smell of new sweat, and left his mind and his mouth to go happily their own way.

She was quite sad when they arrived. She got changed in the disused concrete pillbox that was slipping down the face of the dune into the sea, like all the other girls. It smelled faintly and saltily of urine. But when she got to the edge of the waves, Mick Schneider and Co. were pushing the girls' heads under the water, so she walked along the beach a hundred yards, and swam by herself.

Chapter Four

Wiping her arms with her towel, she made her way back to the door of the pillbox. But one look inside was enough to put her off. Naked legs and boobs and bums filled the pillbox like *The Seraglio* by Ingres, or a mass of wriggling maggots. *The Seraglio* had always reminded her of a mass of wriggling maggots. Girls had certainly changed since she'd left college . . . again, she felt old; about ninety. Though she had always been shy, even at school. She went further up the dune, drying herself carefully and pretending to admire the evening sky, and a solitary flight of ducks. Only when the racket from the pillbox had stopped, and the last girl had left, pinning back her damp hair on the move, with her skirt accidentally caught up in her knickers, did Philippa go in and change. How she loved peace and silence . . . until she saw the name scratched on the pillbox wall.

Cpl C. Smith 22506075 Royal Lancashire Fusiliers.

It couldn't possibly be the same Corporal Smith, Smudger Smith the others called him, thin, under-nourished since a child, with bandy legs under his long khaki shorts and lank black Brylcreemed hair that escaped from his tropical bush-hat at every opportunity. Corporal Smith, who had been detailed to teach her to shoot the revolver. Legs braced well apart, Madam, and both hands on the butt of the weapon. It's got a kick like a mule, Madam, it's much too heavy for you, really, and if you hold it wrong it can break your wrist. But it's the only thing that'll stop them beggars. Don't worry about the foresight, Madam, just point it at the target as you would point your finger at something you were showing somebody. . . .

She saw the gun again, the dull black sheen on it, the brass cartridges in the revolving cylinder. Felt the numbing kick of it; and the terrible bang as it went off . . .

'Philippa?' Brian's voice outside was tentative. Rather as if he was approaching the lair of a rather ill tiger he'd been put in charge of.

The vision of the gun vanished, and she called out, 'Just coming,' with an attempt at false gaiety.

When she emerged, he was standing patiently by his bike. Everybody else was gone. She felt guilty.

'Sorry I kept you waiting. Can we catch them up?'

'I'm not bothered,' he said. 'You can have too much of that lot. Sometimes I get sick of Mike Schneider. I suppose we're too much alike, really.'

'Alike?' He amazed her. 'How, alike?'

'Big,' he said. 'Big and noisy. Got to be the centre of attention all the time. Big he-man stuff.'

'I don't think you're at all like Mick Schneider. You couldn't be more different. You're noisy and nice, and he's noisy and nasty. I wouldn't come swimming with Mick Schneider.'

His face took on an expression of pleased gloom. 'I'm not really noisy, you know. It's all one great big act. Only it fools people, and then you've got to keep up the act, no matter what you really feel like. I'm a quiet, shy person really.'

She had to struggle to keep her face straight. 'You've never struck me as being quiet and shy. I must admit!'

'Well,' he considered. 'There's two me's really. When I'm being noisy and busy, I do quite enjoy it. Though it isn't half exhausting, when you're not feeling up to it. But the other side of me is sort of . . . sad and dreamy. I quite like it, but then I get into it too deep, and can't get out of it, and get really miserable. Really black. Especially when I'm on my own at home in the vac. I sometimes think I'll go mad, till next term comes along and all the people, and that snaps me out of it again. I don't know what would happen if next term didn't turn up.' He stared at the horizon with a very stark and desperate look on his face.

'Don't worry. *You'll* always have people, Brian,' she said, gently. 'People *like* you; girls especially.'

'It's 'cos they know I'm harmless. Like the family dog. I was once crossing Hampstead Heath in the dark with a girl — it was after a party, about two in the morning. And I said to her, wasn't she scared to be out with a bloke in the middle of nowhere at that sort of hour? And she just said no, why should she be? They all think I'm a nice lad, and nobody takes me *seriously*. Why do the rotten bastards get all the girls? I mean, they sort of *fascinate* them . . .'

She gave a little laugh and said, 'You've been watching too many movies, Brian.'

'It's not just the movies. There's a bloke in my college, he's had more girls than I've had hot breakfasts. He drinks like a fish and borrows money off them, and he's lousy to them and they tell me in tears. And then he turns up and crooks his little finger and they're off with him again. Like wasps round a jam-pot. I'd like to smash his face in . . .'

'Go on, you wouldn't hurt a fly . . .'

'I can get bloody rough playing rugger.' He was still

36

staring at the horizon, yearning to find some wickedness inside himself, and only succeeding in looking like a fed-up golden retriever.

She said, rather desperately, 'Like to buy me a drink?'

'I'd like to show you my special place,' he said. 'Where I go when I want to be alone. But I'll buy you a drink after.'

She said, 'A fair bargain,' and he cheered up immediately.

They proceeded at a sedate pace up the coast. The warm dusk was just starting to descend seawards, purpling the waves. Overhead, the swifts were screaming again, in the luminous blue, and to the west, the sunset clouds built up into the castles of childhood you could never hope to reach again. The sound of the waves came to her damp ears faintly, and the chain of his bicycle chirped like a cricket.

'This village is spelt like Happisburgh,' he said. 'But the locals call it Hazebro'. I like to pronounce it Happisburgh myself. Happy town . . . everybody happy all the time.'

'You've got a nice imagination . . .'

'That's what you think. I have very dark thoughts sometimes . . . you've no idea . . . especially about *women*.'

'I shall have to call you the Bad Lord Byron.'

'Stop taking the mickey . . . .' But he giggled, and the bike swerved wildly, and she put a foot to the ground in alarm, and they fell off very slowly, ending in a tangle with the bike on top of them.

'You all right?' he asked anxiously.

'No bones broken. But what'll they think in camp, if I come back with dust and grass all over my skirt?'

'I don't care what they think.'

'Well, I do. Now, please pay attention to what you're doing.'

37

'Yes, Miss!' He joined in dusting the grass off her bottom. But it was all utterly harmless. Like taking a large young dog for a walk.

She could see the tower of Happisburgh church afar off; a huge tall tower, far too big for the church beneath, dominating the low coast. She had imagined he was taking her to some beach, or lonely cove. But now she began to worry he was taking her to the church.

She was terrified of churches now. She was the outcast; she was Cain; she had turned her back on God. Ever since Africa she'd lived with the constant fear that God would strike her dead. Not with a thunderbolt, like in the Old Testament. The New Testament God would be subtler, and use an uncurable disease or a passing bus. But two months had passed now, and God had done nothing. Ignored her. Not even killed their dog at home, or made one of her family ill. But she knew that God was just biding His time. Lurking inside churches like some Heavenly footpad. It was stupid to think He only lurked in churches, but that was how she felt.

She watched the tower, the big plain tower lit orange by the sunset against the purple sky, grow bigger and bigger. She longed to be safe past it. At any moment, they would be past the churchyard gate, and she would let out her breath in a weak laugh, or funny remark.

But he slapped on his brakes. And leaned the bike against the sandstone wall.

'C'mon!'

'I don't much like churches, Brian.'

'What? And you a vicar's daughter. . .'

'Fat lot you know about vicar's daughters . . .'

'Oh, I've heard. They either go one way or the other.'

'What do you mean, one way or the other?'

'Well,' he eyed her with a mixture of shyness and bold-ness. 'They're either very pious – Student Christian Movement and all that, or else they go off the rails completely. Nymphomaniacs. We had one at our college who was *both*. Saturday night and Sunday morning.'

'You men are *vile*!'

'C'mon. I won't let God get you. He's a mate of mine.' He held out a hand to her, like a child. And suddenly she couldn't bear to disappoint him. Oh, well, God, if You're going to get me now, You're going to get me. At least it's in a good cause. Let's get it over with.

But, maddeningly, she had a reprieve. He had to show her all the interesting tombstones first. The man who died at a hundred and two; the seven children of the same family who died before they were ten. The fisherman who was in safe harbour at last. Amidst the long dead grass.

'You're starting to get brown,' he said. 'You look so *alive* against that tombstone.'

She looked at her bare brown arm resting on the old stone.

'You know,' she said, 'I think that's *quite* the nicest compliment anybody's ever paid me.' On the verge of God knew what, she had this absurd desire to giggle.

And then they were inside, and the massive door clanged shut behind her. The same old darkness; same old smell of snuffed wax candles, mouse-dirt, dusty hassocks and incense and Rentokil, which equalled holiness. She looked up the nave and chancel, that great dark tunnel that led to the altar, and she shuddered. God was there, condemning, condemning, condemning. The only thing that was sane was Brian's firm grip, still on her hand.

'C'mon,' he said. 'The best thing's up here.' He began to

drag her towards the altar. She felt that the life was draining from her brain, her arms, her legs, into a little pool in the centre of her, round her vulnerable beating heart that could stop any moment and drop her into the pit of Hell. She started the same old pathetic pleading within herself. I didn't mean to do it. It wasn't meant to be that way, it wasn't meant to be that way at all . . . all useless, of course. What all the killers said, when they were dragged to justice. What that French Bluebeard Landru who had murdered dozens of women must have gibbered, as they rushed him to the guillotine.

Then another reprieve, stuck half-way up the aisle.

'You know,' said Brian, putting on his grave philosophical voice. 'I sometimes wonder if we've got God the wrong way round.'

'What *do* you mean?' She had the impression neither her eyes nor her ears were working properly any more.

'Well, the big question is, did God make man, or man make God?'

'Brian, for Heaven's sake . . .'

'Well, take this church. Who made it? Men. Who prays in it? Men . . . and women and children, of course. Who put all the fancy decorations in it? Men. Who are all these memorials to? Men. Who brings the stuff for the Harvest Festival? Men. I mean, it's like building a great big dog kennel and putting a pup in it. Then you feed the pup, and are nice to it, and it gets bigger and bigger, and pretty fierce. And then the kennel's a safe place to leave your valuables, because the pup will guard them. And so the kennel gets more and more precious, and the pup more and more important, till your whole life is filled serving the pup.'

'What precious things is your pup supposed to be guarding here, Brian?' She had never heard anything so crazy in her life, and yet from one point of view, it made sense. If you started from the other end, from scratch.

'Well, my Mum and Dad are pretty precious to me. And if they died, I'd want to know where they were, so I could come back and see them. I mean, if they were cremated and the ashes scattered, they wouldn't be *anywhere* would they? And I couldn't bear that. Whereas if they were buried here, with a nice stone, under a shady tree or something, and I knew God was looking after them, that would be quite bearable, wouldn't it?'

His face was beseeching, pleading for her to understand. 'I mean, this place is the memory of the whole . . . district. It sort of holds space and time together. War memorials . . . girl guide banners . . . stained glass windows given in memory of . . . it would be . . . impossible, if it was ever pulled down. It would be a desert, and everyone would be lost.'

'I don't think that will ever happen, Brian.'

'It could. If people lost faith in the pup. If people stopped looking after it, it would die and the dog kennel would fall to bits. Some of these churches round here . . . you should see the state of them, the cracks in the walls, the slates off the roofs. Look what happened to the monasteries . . . '

'You're talking like an atheist, Brian. Like Karl Marx. "Religion is the opium of the people . . . " '

'No, no, *no*.' He did a curious little dance of frustration and exasperation on the stone floor-flags. 'I'm not an atheist just now, though I have been quite often in my life, I'm not *now*. I know there's something here in this church. And we *need* it. We'd be lost without it. Can't you *feel* it?'

'Yes,' she said. 'Yes, I can.' And shuddered.

'But when this place was just a turnip field, before the church was built, it wasn't here then. Men *brought* it.'

'Where from?'

'Another church? Stonehenge or something. It's still there at Stonehenge. I felt it.'

'Oh, Brian, Brian! You've got my mind in a whirl. I don't know where I am with you. I can't keep up with you.'

'Come and light a candle with me.' He led the way to a black, ugly, wrought-iron candlestand, hung with stalactites of old candle-grease. There was an open wooden box of thin candles below, and a closed box, with a slot, for the money.

'One for you, and one for me, and one for me Mum, and one for me Dad.' He jammed them in one after the other. 'Anybody else you want to light one for?'

Trembling, she picked out four candles of her own. Her hand was shaking so much, she had trouble getting them into the holders. In the end he had to help her. Then he solemnly handed her a twopenny box of matches from an iron tray at one side.

'You can light mine too, if you like,' he said, gallantly.

They looked back as they left the church.

'They look like stars in the dark,' she said.

'Well, the pup's got his dinner tonight!'

'Oh, Brian, you are *awful*!'

But riding home through the dusk without lights; in the strange pub where there was nobody but themselves and the landlord and two old men playing dominoes, she felt strangely at ease. She had lit candles for dead faces, and not been struck dead.

Maybe, she thought, this Pup was Something you truly might one day possibly learn to live with.

Maybe she would escape, tonight, the terrible shapeless

42

dreams that left her gasping and shaking when she wakened in the morning.

Chapter Five

When they got back, the whole camp was very quiet. The Shed was in darkness. They had taken a long time getting from the pub without lights.

'God, it's gone eleven,' whispered Brian. 'I'll be *dead* in the morning. Goodnight.' And he moved away along the men's tents, the only noise the swish of his footsteps on the grass, and the tiny chirr of his freewheel.

Suddenly, his whispering made her feel furtive. Well, not furtive, just frightened of waking people up. As she made her own way, she became aware of gentle female snores, but also of listening ears too perhaps . . . the tents loomed up like pale pyramids in the dark.

There was still a glimmer of light in the last tent, hers. Brod must have turned the wick of the lamp down low and left it for her to get undressed by. That was kind.

Brod seemed to be asleep; her face did not look innocent, as so many faces looked innocent in sleep, even old people's. She looked like a disgruntled baby, forced to sleep with a grudge against the world, who might wake up and howl at any moment . . . Philippa began to undress silently.

And then caught the tiniest glint from Brod's eyes. Brod was watching her get undressed, through lowered lids. There seemed a kind of malicious greed in her watchfulness, which Philippa found unbearable.

'Are you awake?' she said softly. 'Sorry if I wakened you.' She was still hoping it was a trick of the low lamplight. Some people sleep with their eyes not quite shut . . . she so much didn't want Brod to wake up, and spoil her calm before sleep.

But the next instant, Brod's eyes flicked wide open. And the greedy malice was still there, only more so now.

'You got what you wanted, then?' said Brod. 'Congratulations.' The sarcasm was heavy, and laden with innuendo. Philippa's mood rocketed from peace to instant rage.

'What do you mean, what I *wanted*?' She still kept her voice down to a hiss.

'Oh, don't try to come the innocent. Don't tell me you two were only waiting for the moon to rise . . .'

'Brian took me to see a church he'd found. Then we went to a pub . . .' Then she felt angry with herself for saying anything. What right had Brod to know where she'd been?

'Church? Pub? Till this time? With all those lovely haystacks and hedgerows about? Try pulling the other leg, it's got bells on it.'

A sudden, silly panic clutched at Philippa's guts, a conviction that this would be all over the camp tomorrow, and the campers would believe Brod's smeary version. And it was Brian's good name as well as her own. . . .

'I can assure you we were only talking . . .'

'No need to get hoity-toity with me, chum. Trying to prove you're a cut above the common herd? Talking about *what*?'

'God, actually . . .' Funny, with the mention of God, contempt crept into her voice.

For the first time, Brod looked shaken. 'God? Blokes only have one God, and it hangs between their legs.'

'Brian's not like that.'

'Brian? I can almost believe it. Brian *would* be a slow worker. I know his sort. Talk about God, and the Meaning of Life, I suppose. Stun the woman with the depth of his intellect, then start groping up her skirt while she's still anaesthetised by his brilliance. Yes, that sounds like our Brian. All appealing, like a puppy-dog.'

'I think you *stink*.'

'Too near the mark, was it?'

'If you think I'm that sort . . .'

'Oh, there are two sorts, are there? Ladies and *women?*'

'Just shut *up*!' Philippa could not keep any of the disgust and, yes . . . real hate . . . out of her voice.

It served to silence Brod, who rolled over with a great angry heave, leaving a view of her back that was like a shaken fist.

Philippa, remorse-stricken, knew there was no mending this; she had made an enemy for life.

It was a long time before either of them slept. Every grunt and sigh was like a starshell exploding over a battlefield.

She wakened up with the first of the sun through the tent flap. Her dreams had been just as exhausting, as usual, but different, somehow, though she could not remember any details, as usual. What she knew for a certainty was that there would be no getting back to sleep. She was wide awake, painfully wide awake. Heat was starting to build up as the sun fell on the tent walls, and Brod's snoring was oppressive, as if she was carrying on the war even in sleep.

She got up and dressed quickly. Grabbed her sponge-bag and towel and was out. She walked along the line of tents feeling utterly lonely. The cool flow of the dew through the open fronts of her sandals, the singing of the birds, the smell of fresh greenery mocked her. She looked at her watch. Half past five. More than an hour before the camp wakened up. Well, thank God for small mercies. Though how she was going to face them all over breakfast, when Brod's tongue would certainly get wagging, and the covert glances would start . . .

She needed . . . someone. Not Brian, because that would only make the gossip worse. But someone.

At one time she would have prayed, God, send me someone. A little silent arrow-prayer silently up from the top of her head. But God was the Enemy now. And you never asked the Enemy favours.

She turned into the women's wash tent; the standpipe-tap and long wooden-slat tables, with their rows of enamel bowls.

There was somebody else there, in the sudden gloom at the far end. Somebody slight and shy and nervous.

A tall thin girl she'd noticed round the Shed. A girl who would have been graceful, but for the fact that she hunched her back and drooped her head, trying to conceal her height. Blue eyes, pale lips, long beautiful hair that badly needed a wash. A pale, diffident, placatory, failure of a smile.

An outsider, who sat at the ends of dinner-tables, trying to get into the boisterous meal-conversations and failing. Philippa had an idea she'd come with a noisier, more confident friend, but that the friend had abandoned her for a bloke. She felt a twinge of shame at her own selfish self-pity. There were more outsiders than she in the camp; more reasons for being outside than being older and a bit prim. So she went out of her way to be nice.

'Isn't it lovely to have the place to ourselves? All that racket! And isn't the early morning beautiful?'

The girl only nodded; but her second attempt at a smile succeeded. Then she ducked away again, sloshing water onto her face from the basin. Like a little rabbit.

Philippa deliberately walked closer and picked up the enamel basin next to the girl, whereas before she'd have stuck to the far corner. She filled the bowl with cold water, and walked back, and threw her stuff down next to the girl's, companionably. The child buried her face into her towel with another flurry; but not a rejecting flurry. There was a little colour in her cheeks now.

'D'you find your back aches in the mornings?' asked Philippa.

'Not much, no.'

'Oh, what it is to be young!'

'My knees ache a bit. But it wears off.'

'What you on?'

'Gooseberries. My arms are scratched to bits.'

'Long-sleeved shirt helps.'

'Hadn't thought of that. I've only brought one. But I think I'll try it. You seem to have escaped.'

They sploshed away companionably. Philippa felt a little better. This was a nice child.

'D'you like picking?'

'It's all right, I suppose. It's a bit boring, with no one to talk to.'

'Haven't you got a partner?'

'No.' The girl's voice faltered. Her shoulders dropped. She sounded lonely, even homesick.

'I'd rather be alone than have mine,' said Philippa. 'She never stops grumbling. Bitch, bitch, bitch.'

'I know the sort,' said the girl, fumbling with her wet soap, but with a wild tinge of hope in her voice.

'Would you mind very much if you and I worked together today?'

'Oh, I'd like that,' said the girl, turning towards Philippa, her face suddenly alive. How sad, thought Philippa; how loneliness and strangeness can mar such a lovely face, turn it to a frozen mask of misery, drain it of all life.

'Well, if we stick together, they're bound to choose us.' Then she took a deep breath and said, 'Fancy a walk before breakfast? Work up an appetite?'

'Yes, please!'

By the time they reached the still-sleeping village, the child was bubbling over with enthusiasm. Every flower, every dew-laden spider's web seemed to please her. She rattled out her life. She was called Sonia Birtwisle and she was a first-year art student at Newcastle. She liked tennis; Daddy was teaching her to play tennis. Daddy still loomed very important in her life. And the dog, and the cat and . . .

At that point, as they neared the cinder-track to the camp, Philippa, who had been content to listen, suddenly tensed. There were two figures standing in the middle of the narrow road in front, with bowed heads, and one of them, by far the larger, was Brian. Embarrassment made her voice too loud.

'What on earth are you two doing?'

Brian looked up. 'Snail crossing the road,' he said. 'We're giving it an escort, in case it gets flattened.'

It was a very large, sedate snail, a Roman snail. They all stood around, watching its slow progress.

'I don't know why they have to cross roads,' said Brian. 'What impulse drives them? The grass on that side looks just as green as the grass this side. . . .'

'If you're so worried about it,' said Philippa, 'why don't you just pick it up, and carry it before you miss breakfast?'

'That would be interfering unwarrantably with nature,' said the second man. 'According to Brian, that is.' He had a humorous voice, very Northern Irish.

'This is Trev,' said Brian. 'He sleeps with me. But only platonically. . . .'

'I'm studying the English snore for my thesis,' said Trev, 'and Brian was too good a subject to miss. He also talks to someone called Lady Julia in his sleep, though awake he denies all knowledge of her. A fascinating nut-case. I'd like to take him back to Belfast and dissect him.' He was small and pale, with freckles and flaming red hair. For harvest camp he was dressed rather formally, a smart sports coat above his khaki shorts, and the collar of his khaki shirt turned down neatly outside his coat-lapels.

'This is Sonia Birtwisle . . .'

'Hi, Sonia.' Trev grinned, and Sonia grinned back at him.

'Bless you, my children,' said Brian. 'I now declare you man and wife.'

Everybody laughed, but Brian fell in beside Philippa, and Trev beside Sonia behind, and they returned to the camp a faction that was to survive to the end. They even had the nerve to occupy the centre table for breakfast that was normally reserved for the camp characters.

Philippa stretched full-length to pick the last gooseberry, and, irrationally, popped it into her mouth. It was ripe and soft and fairly sweet. Gooseberries didn't show up in your mouth like blackcurrants, and besides, this farmer wasn't so mean and tight. Down the row, Brian and Trev and Sonia had fallen silent at last, a comfortable grunting silence, with an occasional sound of Sonia humming to herself.

The last four days had passed so fast for the four of them. They always worked together now. Brian had a certain pull with the farmers, that made it possible. And their running fantasies made the hours fly. The fantasy that Trev was really a leprechaun, and attended not Queen's University, Belfast, but the Royal College of Leprechauns, where they did Ph.D.s in subjects like using your knife and fork. The fantasy that Sonia was really a Russian spy (well, she had to be with a name like Sonia), and her very Englishness was proof of what a good spy she was, and there was a bloke back in the Kremlin waiting eagerly for the blackcurrant production figures of the Norfolk fruit farms. That Philippa was secretly training to be the first woman archbishop. . . .

Philippa stretched in the sun, and yawned like a cat. She was one of four now, and in four was safety . . . safety from camp gossip, safety from the memories of the mission station. She washed, ate, worked, washed again, ate, swam, drank in the pub. Every hot day passed like every other hot day; she lived in her hands and her skin and her belly, skimming over the black depths of the past like a water-boatman skims a pond.

She and Brod no longer spoke. It would have been easier for them both if one of them could've moved tents, but every tent was full. But when you had a gang, the tent hardly mattered. It was only when you were new, lonely, homesick, that the tent seemed a home, a refuge. Now it was just a place where you slept and went to get changed and the whole warm open-air width of Norfolk was your home.

There had been one attack from Brod. As Philippa blew out the light one night, she said from her bed,

'You think you've been ever so clever, don't you?' Well, more *spat* it out, actually. The problem of Brod was still there, and getting more insoluble all the time. But the sun was warm, and they'd go bathing tonight, and then the pub . . .

She had the slight surprising thought that maybe there *was* life after the mission station, the dead face.

'Pack up. Paaack uuuup!' The welcome call came down the lines of bushes.

Chapter Six

They lay in the hayfield after lunch. Haymaking was light work, little more than a lark. Raking the cut hay into long rows down the field. Forking it up into the haywain where Trev, still neat in his sports coat, tried to trample it down into a safe load for the journey back to the barn. While they bombarded him with hay, trying to knock him off the top; and drawing frantic yells when a well-aimed shot sent a shower of hayseeds down inside his shirt.

They were in a good mood. The farmer (who, as usual, was a mate of Brian's) had been generous with dark beer-bottles of cold tea, and huge slices of home-baked apple-pie at lunchtime, to augment their usual wretched Spam sandwiches.

They lay in a pattern that had started as a joke, but had persisted. Philippa used Brian's tummy as a pillow, Sonia used Philippa's tummy as a pillow, and Trev used Sonia. It was hilarious, because every time Brian laughed he made Philippa's head bounce up and down . . . it was a joke they never tired of. But there was pleasure for Philippa beyond that. The steady thump of Brian's heart sounding in her ear, reassuring as the tick of a grandfather clock; the sweet smell of his new sweat, the steady rise and fall of his breathing, his occasional sighs. She had never in all her life been so close to anyone (certainly never Max). But she thought it as harmless and natural a pleasure as the smell of Sonia's newly-washed hair, and the feel of it under her fingers. It all brought such safety, such a feeling of not being alone in the world.

'This camp is a non-stop place for laughs,' said Sonia contentedly, full of lunch. 'Those Basques . . . I asked one of them what he was doing last night and he said, "In my tent, I was *leaping*".'

'He meant "sleeping",' said Trev, pedantically.

'Oh, for God's sake, don't spoil the image,' said Brian. 'It's a lovely picture, a tent full of bouncing Basques, all in mid-flight. Like the Festival Ballet, or a cage full of monkeys.'

'You're a true poet, Brian,' said Trev. 'You're wasted on chemistry.'

'The *really* weird one,' said Brian, 'is Sadnicki. He wants to wrestle with me all the time. Keeps on leaping on my back, out of dark corners. Without warning.'

'Maybe he fancies you?'

'It's not funny. I'm twice his size, but he always wins. I always end up flat on my face with my arm twisted up behind my ear. He's *mad*.'

'He's very handsome,' said Sonia, 'with that crew-cut and big moustache.'

'I want a *divorce*,' said Trev. 'Anyway, he *is* totally barmy. He gets up at five every morning, to practice his knife-throwing. He's got this deadly-looking thing in a sheath behind his neck, under his shirt. He practices for three hours, till breakfast-time. And he can throw that knife ten yards and put it straight through an inch-thick plank. The camp notice-board by his tent is dissolving into splinters. He's *lethal*. He's going to end up killing somebody, if he doesn't watch it.'

'He's waiting for the Russians to invade,' said Sonia solemnly, 'so he can kill them all. He told me.'

'Why does he want to kill the Russians?'

'Because they betrayed him and his friends in the Warsaw Uprising. The Russians were ten miles from Warsaw in 1944, when the Polish Resistance rose against the Nazis. He says the Russians just sat there, ten miles away, until the Nazis wiped the whole Resistance out.'

'But that was eight years ago – he'd only have been a kid . . . pull the other leg, it's got bells on it.'

'He says he was only eleven at the time, and very small – he was a messenger and he was so small the Nazis didn't bother to shoot at him.'

There was a long and thoughtful silence. Then Trev said, 'Oh, come on, you can't believe everything people tell you at harvest camp. Nobody knows the truth about anybody else. They can get away with telling whoppers. I mean, how much do even us here know about each other?'

'Well, we know Sonia's a Russian spy. What else could she be, with a name like Sonia?'

'Actually, I'm head of the Far Eastern branch of the Jehovah's Witnesses . . .'

'Out to conquer the universe, I suppose,' said Trev, banging his head up and down on her stomach. 'Naughty girl!'

'Philippa's the real dark horse,' said Brian. 'Her suitcase was so heavy she has to have a radio-transmitter in it.'

'Come on, Philippa,' said Sonia, banging her head up and down on Philippa's stomach in turn. 'Spill the beans. What were you doing before you came to this harvest camp?'

It was utterly horrible. The silence while they all waited for her to speak. The sun was still warm and comforting on her face, but her friends had turned into Inquisitors;

Inquisitors so close they could feel every tremor of her body. And behind her closed lids (through which the red sunlight leaked a little) the dead face of Max swam up to her. She wanted to scream; if she so much as clenched her hand they would notice. But she held on to her nerve by her finger-nails, and let one phrase come to her help . . . Spill the beans . . .

'You've heard of Heinz 57 varieties? Well, I'm research-ing the 58th. Frog's legs in honey sauce. And after that, frogspawn in cream. It's us that's going to conquer the universe . . .'

'God,' said Trev. '*Another* mad scientist! Why do we never get mad *artists*?'

'Who'd be afraid of a mad artist?'

'All artists are mad. Otherwise they wouldn't be artists . . .'

And so they trailed on with their silly fantasies and she was safe again. Until Brian said, 'The really baffling guy is Sam Otenbe. I mean, we live like pigs in tents, but every evening he turns out in immaculate white collar and tie, blazer and white flannels. How does he *do* it?'

'Well, he's a Kenyan – a Kikuyu. They're used to living in mud huts.'

'Kikuyu are the Mau Mau, aren't they? The ones who are busy chopping up the white settlers with pangas.' Sonia's voice was hushed and horrified.

'Most of the Kikuyu are decent law-abiding people,' said Philippa, through stiff lips. 'They are more afraid of the Mau Mau than anybody. They're the ones who suffer most, not the white families. Thousands of Kikuyu have been killed by the Mau Mau.'

There was another long unbearable silence. Then Sonia said, 'I don't believe Sam Otenbe would chop anybody up.

He's so gentle. He's got a lovely smile. He held my hand in the pub last night and said, "Fly with me to the Antipodes . . ."'

'Oh, he says that to all the girls. That's the joke . . .'

'I think he's *sweet*,' said Sonia stoutly.

He seems very sweet, thought Philippa. But how do we know? How can we know what goes on behind that smiling face, and a perfect imitation of the white man's uniform? How can we ever know about any of them?

She shuddered.

'Somebody walk over your grave, Philippa?' asked Brian.

Not over *my* grave. But maybe Max's grave . . . She began to sweat and it wasn't with the heat.

'I like him better than that Ade Tshombe,' said Sonia. 'With all his talk of his father being a chief in Nigeria who just happens to have forgotten to send him his allowance this month . . . he borrows money off all the men, and gets drunk on it every night. *And* he made a pass at me, when Trev's back was turned. A really heavy pass. Hand up my blouse . . .'

'Why didn't you tell me?' asked Trev, fiercely. 'When was this? Where was this?'

'In the cookhouse, washing up. I hit him over the head with a frying pan, hard, and he slid down the wall like a broken doll, and said, "You only did that to me because I am black." And I said, "I'll do it to anybody. I don't care if they're black, white or sky-blue-pink, nobody's going to do anything to me I don't want done".'

'Good for you,' said Philippa.

Trev said thoughtfully, 'All the white students think they're being so liberal . . . the men lend them money and never get it back, and the girls get pregnant. What's so liberal about that?'

'Oh, for God's sake, let's talk about something else,' said Philippa. 'This is supposed to be a holiday.'

But for the rest of the afternoon, the golden English hayfield was the dusty plain of Africa. She knew now she'd never get away from it.

Chapter Seven

Brian asked her to work, that Saturday morning. It was a perk he'd grabbed as Camp Chairman, for at the weekend the farmer paid time and a half. And it was carefree because they'd knock off at twelve and miss the heat of the day. And they'd have the whole glorious empty weekend in front of them. She rode up to the farm on his cross-bar; there seemed no other way of travelling now.

The job was light and interesting; stooking corn. The old horse-drawn reaper-and-binder spewed out a succession of tied sheaves. She and Brian each picked up a pair of warm, rustling tickling sheaves and tucked one under each armpit. Then they faced each other, like partners in some ancient rustic open-air dance. In turn (and this was the tricky bit, but Brian had shown her how) they banged their sheaves together and downward, so that the heavy heads of corn mingled inextricably. Then they gingerly leaned their joined pairs together, as if they were bowing to each other, and the new stook stood upright and four-square on its own, safe from the damp and mildew of the stubble. There was a trick to it, but she had learnt the trick easily, and was full of childish delight at her new skill, as they added further pairs to each end of the stook, making eight in all.

'Like making little marriages,' Brian said. 'Corn-marriages. The corn-bride and the corn-groom.' He grinned his private inward grin, pleased at the ingenuity of his own idea.

'What about all the other sheaves?' She could not resist pricking his innocent bubble, setting him off, seeing that frown of thought grow on his sunburnt brow.

'Corn-bridesmaids, corn-mums, corn-dads. It's all very Anglo-Saxon, somehow.'

'Why Anglo-Saxon? Didn't the Normans grow corn?' Oh, she knew what he meant, right enough, when he said Anglo-Saxon. The goldenness of the corn, the goldenness of his hair, now bleaching with the sun, the deeper brown-gold of his face and heavy arms, the golden dryness of the whole bleached field, only relieved by certain stalks in the stubble that, full of overnight dew, shot delicious cool jets of water up your bare legs as you trod on them. The Anglo-Saxons had loved corn and gold . . . the gold that Beowulf died for. Gold torcs and Danegeld.

But she had this need to tease him now, shoot probing questions at him, shake him, watch his blue eyes cloud over with thought, before the next bright wild answer popped out of his mouth. He was like a child let loose in a world that was full of wondrous toys, that he picked up and played with and dropped. Marxism and Existentialism, the Holy Grail and the action of thermals on sailplanes. Now he said, eyes wide with enthusiasm,

'Haven't you heard of corn-dollies? The Anglo-Saxons used to choose and sacrifice a young harvest-king and harvest-queen, to ensure the next year's harvest with their blood. They used to plough their bodies into the furrows, the following spring. Then they got a bit more civilised and used figures plaited from corn instead. They still make little corn-dollies round here; but they're only for the tourist-trade now.'

'Can't have been a lot of fun for the harvest-king and harvest-queen!'

'I don't know – they had their season. Summer and autumn and winter. They were treated like a real king and queen, while they lived. No rotten old back-breaking work and going hungry. Making love all over the place and the more they made love, the more the people approved. They had each other, like nobody else had; with no one to stop them. And a quick end. No lingering on to get old and toothless and rheumaticky and die of starvation . . . then the Church came and buggered it up.'

'You don't like the church, do you, Brian?'

'I only like churches when they're empty. The moment the vicar shows up, I'm off. They always start off by being matey and as real as a three-pound note. Then they start getting at you, to make you feel guilty, and once they've made you feel guilty, they've got you for life.'

In a sudden darkness, Philippa remembered Max. How well Brian had summed up Max, and his Kingdom of Guilt. Max wouldn't have got far with Brian, and for some reason that made Brian very wonderful.

'The Church didn't get far round here,' said Brian, cutting through her darkness with cheerful incomprehension. 'With the East Angles of East Anglia, I mean. They had a King – King Anna. The first Christian missionary got him worried with tales of hell-fire. So he built a double-church with two altars – one to God and one to Odin; a sort of double death-insurance. Whichever turned out to be true – Heaven or Valhalla, King Anna was fireproof. And when he made all his warriors get baptised by total immersion in the river, they always held their sword-arms above the water, because their sword-arms were dedicated to Odin . . .'

He gave the wickedest chuckle she'd ever heard him give. Then his expression changed and he said,

'Ey, we must get on. This farmer's a mate of mine, and he *is* paying us time and a half.'

For the rest of that morning, under the weight of the sun on her back and the songs of the larks, she thought about the harvest king and harvest queen, with all their happiness rolled up short into one season. Living like the bright dragon-flies, heedless of their end . . . .

Suddenly it seemed possible that she might live like that, for this short summer of camp, ignoring the darkness beyond, being just happy. If she *dared*.

Suddenly, she thought she might dare. If her end was to be dreadful anyway . . . why not?

It was as if a little spring of life was released inside her. Suddenly it was possible to be happy again. Not yet the end, not yet.

She straightened up, with her hands to her back, and looked up into the pale blue sky, and the feeling was glorious.

They cycled back towards the camp. She was very good on the cross-bar now. She'd lost all her nervousness and they swayed in unison round the corners, so they were able to go much faster.

She felt . . . dried out. She'd stopped sweating hours ago. Brian said it was because her body knew it couldn't afford to sweat any more. And she felt bleached by the sun, burned away. Only dry skin and bone, like that pre-historic Egyptian sand-mummy in the British museum who had blessedly died before there was even Moses to worry about, let alone Jesus. Buried with only a few pots of food for the journey to the hereafter, without the blessings or cursings of Mother Church. Lucky, lucky mummy . . . .

'We could do with a drink,' muttered Brian into her ear, and cycled up to the Pleasure Boat, arriving tempestuously in an explosion of flying gravel, to scattered cheers from the students.

She went and sat down inside, glad of the sudden sooty dark, and the coolness of the chair. Brian went straight to the bar; he knew what she liked to drink now. She just sat, eyes shut, her arms rejoicing in the iciness of the marble table-top. She heard him come back, and felt him place her glass against the ends of her fingertips, so that she could drink it without opening her eyes.

'Cheers,' said Brian, in an amused, expectant voice.

She picked up her half-pint of cider, took a mouthful, and then found she couldn't stop drinking, even to breathe. Her throat just ran away with her; it seemed to have a tearing, ravenous life of its own, like a beast of prey.

The next second, she felt sweat break out from every pore of her body. Like a wave. Torrential, ridiculous sweat like she had never known even in Africa. But unlike the long slow misery of African sweat, this was like . . . she had a silly image of Botticelli's *Venus* rising naked and lovely from the waves. It was delicious sweat, that galloped away with her, out of control, like a bolting horse. Her body was an omnipotent queen, and her tiny worrying mind was utterly silenced. She had never had such pleasure from her body; it was embarrassing, but she didn't care. She thought, I'm turning into an animal, and I don't care.

She opened her eyes to see Brian grinning at her. He was sweating in exactly the same way.

'Funny, isn't it? The body just decides it's ready to go. It

63

only happens with a cool drink, in a cool place. I wouldn't miss it. I look forward to it.'

She wiped drips of sweat off the tip of her nose, as they began to fall on the marble-topped table. 'You did that to me deliberately. You *knew* it was going to happen. Who gave you the right . . .?'

But she couldn't really be angry; the way he was grinning in triumph, he looked about five years old. So she kicked him on the shin instead. Three times. But gently.

'You've got yourself a handful there, Brian,' somebody called from the end of the bar. But there was no harm in it. And already his butterfly mind was off on another tack.

'It's the big trip tonight. To the haunted mill. Midnight picnic. I've got the cook to make us some smashing cakes. It's a sort of institution, the trip to the mill. Annual event. Sometimes we're hours finding it. Sometimes we can't find it at all. It only lets itself be found when it *wants* to be found . . .'

'Tripe, Trench. Kids' stuff. Enid Blyton!' The jeering voice came from a distance.

Peering down the long bar, she saw Mick Schneider lounging with his huge arm round a girl. He was treating the girl like a plaything, squeezing her painfully, even reaching up to fondle her breast in public. The students sitting around were trying not to look. But the girl seemed to be loving it, wriggling and giggling, silly little thing.

Then she saw who the girl was. Brod.

'Let's go somewhere where the air's fresher,' said Brian, getting to his feet abruptly. His big hands were trembling on the table and she knew it wasn't with fear.

She got up without a word; and the rest of the students inside got up to follow them.

64

More raucous bellows from Mick, and the shrill giggles of Brod, followed them out into the open air.

The real trouble started at supper-time in the Shed. Mick and Brod had brought their raucous conspiracy with them, ruining everybody's excitement at the evening ahead. Mick kept leaning over and putting his huge hands on Brod's bare thighs, and it was quite enough to drive the rest away to arm's length, even their usual acquaintances.

It was odd, thought Philippa, the conventions among students. They debated endlessly about Free Love, but in public they were oddly chaste. There was plenty of hand-holding between couples at the camps, but that seemed to be all, apart from long goodnight-kissing sessions at tent doors. You might ask what they got up to in private, but they seemed to choose to have very little privacy, in spite of the endless fields and woods around them. They went around in fours or sixes or twenties and thirties, as activities and alliances changed. Was it morality that held them back, she wondered? Or the fact that contraceptives were only available from dirty old news-vendors at football queues, or dirty-minded barbers who offered young men their wares to raise a laugh, in front of a guffawing crowd of cronies? Or was it that getting a girl pregnant meant giving up college and taking some wretched clerking job to support her and a squalling brat in two squalid rooms, with all hope of a degree and a career gone?

Or was it that feeling that sex-all-the-way had a darkness in it? That girls who did it, even if they didn't get pregnant, found their concentration gone, and their work going to pieces, and started hanging round the cloakrooms for hours in tears, and frequently departed at the end of term, never to return. Perhaps the estate of student, on a government grant, with National Service to come for the men, was too frail an estate to support anything more than a goodnight kiss. Students were butterflies, happy butterflies, and content to remain so.

Terry rose at the end of the meal; at his most ecclesiastical.

'About the trip to the haunted mill tonight . . . we aim to start at eleven after the pub shuts. Anyone with a basket on their bike who can carry goodies for us, please let me know. And . . . bottles of cider, but nothing stronger, please!'

'Gnat's piss!' shouted Mick.

Terry went pale, but decided to ignore him. 'You'll probably find it worth while to take a warm woolly – it gets pretty cold after midnight.'

'And don't forget to take spare underpants,' shouted Mick. 'In case you see a ghostie!'

Terry hovered, clinging onto his clipboard like a drowning sailor clings to a raft.

Philippa felt Brian, beside her, lurch to his feet.

'Look, Schneider, if you don't want to come, that's all right by me. But just stay out of it. Don't spoil things for the people who do.'

'Who made you the boss? Who gave you the right to tell other people what to do, Trench?'

'I happen to have been voted Camp Chairman.'

'Oh, big *deal*!'

'I'm calling for another vote. I propose this trip to the mill is by invitation only.'

'Seconded! ' said Trev.

'Thirded,' said another man, and got a laugh. It was a nervous laugh, but oddly aggressive.

'Those in favour?' asked Brian.

Every girl's hand went up except Brod's.

And all but three of the men, who were, or had been, cronies of Mick.

'Those against?'

Mick and Brod, and that was all.

'Motion carried by thirty-eight to two, with three abstentions. You're not invited, Mick. Nor your woman.'

'England's a free country. We can do what we like.'

'Try it, chum. Just try it . . .'

That was the first time Philippa felt a twinge of fear. So, obviously, did Terry. He said, desperately,

'Well if that's democratically settled . . .'

'F— off,' said Mick, walking out, followed by Brod.

Everyone went down to the pub that night in a great big group. There was no sign of Mick and Brod, and everyone breathed a sigh of relief. But they were still tense, which was perhaps why they drank a little more than usual, sang a bit louder than usual. Things got a bit riotous, with the camp characters wandering from table to table. The Basques did a traditional song and dance, or so they said. It seemed to largely consist of punching each other and giving ceiling-cracking whoops. Sadnicki kept buttonholing people and asking them if they thought Mick was a Nazi, in a sinisterly hopeful sort of way. Sam Otenbe asked more girls than usual to fly with him to the Antipodes. For once, even the pub landlord was sweating, and his wall-to-wall grin was looking a little worn.

But it was Ade Tshombe who was the real pain in the backside. Too much beer made him belch repeatedly, and he was clever at turning his belches into words, or even phrases 'OOOOOOxford won the Boat Race,' and 'GGGGOD save the Queen, GOOOOOD bless her.' It got a few laughs, but not many. So he turned his next few belches into 'MAU MAU'. 'MAU MAU' he belched, over and over. That created a great silence; it was too much even for the student liberal conscience; out in Kenya, too many people had died. Old ladies; children; white children. It was not *any* kind of joke.

In the end, Sadnicki, only slightly less drunk, lurched up to him.

'I think the Mau Mau are black Nazis,' he said. 'Nazis with black skins. There are too many Nazis left in the world.'

Even Ade Tshombe, drunk as he was, saw the warning lights. He went pale, from near-black, it seemed, to a rather unhealthy shade of khaki. From being aggressive, he went into his pathetic stance. Laid his hand perilously on Sadnicki's chest and said, solemn as an owl:

'My dear friend, Mau Mau is an invention of the English gutter press. There is no such organisation as Mau Mau.'

Sadnicki did not take this well. He stood as stiff as a ramrod, with his hair and huge moustache bristling in an unearthly way. Then he flicked Ade's hand away as he might flick a fly, and went out onto the riverbank, and began throwing his knife at an inoffensive lifebelt on a post. Ade, suddenly feeling alone and in need of friends, began going from group to group, laying his hands on the mens' chests and repeating solemnly over and over

'There is no such organisation as Mau Mau.'

But for once he had gone too far. Student liberalism, on which he 'had so long depended, which he had so long abused, had been stretched too far, and snapped. They were tired of making allowances, lending money on wild promises, being fumbled sexually in a good cause. He suddenly became a revolting object who nobody wanted to know. As group after group gently pushed him away (for they still kept their manners), he grew very frightened. And his look of fear was reflected in the face of his friend, Sam Otenbe. Philippa looked at Sam's good-natured face, and could have wept for him.

And for herself, pressing remorselessly down every minute of every day. The black resentment hiding behind smiling, fawning imitation, but growing, growing. Then, inevitably, the violence. The hot violence of the whites. The coffined, bewildered faces of the white dead; the lines of black Mau Mau bodies, laid out for inspection in the broiling sun as if they were shot deer or pheasant. A good bag this time, sir!

'Man, I tell you, I assure you, there is no such organisation as Mau Mau.' His voice seemed to ring on and on through Philippa's head. She looked at her hands on the table-top and they were visibly shaking. She pressed them hard down to stop them.

'You OK?' asked Brian, coming back with more drinks.

'It's hot in here,' she said, and cursed herself for a coward. For his response was inevitable.

'Let's go for a walk to the end of the jetty.' He took her arm and practically hauled her to her feet, so she didn't have to make any decision.

The air outside was much cooler, and it was nice as the din fell away, and there was just the sound of water lapping, and the ropes of the yachts rattling against their masts in the light breeze off the Broad.

But her problems were not over. She could not stop shaking. She could not think of anything to say to the three concerned faces peering at her in the gloom. The silence seemed to go on and on, and in the end it seemed simpler just to lean in towards Brian and rest her burning face against his chest. He put his great arms around her, and felt her trembling and said,

'It's something serious, isn't it?'

He *cared*. They all cared. They deserved to know *something*. She took a deep breath and said,

'I've just come back from Kenya. I knew some people who were killed by the Mau Mau. The whole family. I was very fond of them. Sorry!'

Sorry for being a wet blanket. Sorry for ruining their evening.

'Christ,' said Brian. She thought that for a person of his strange beliefs, he used that word awfully often. 'Hey, Trev go and tell Sam Otenbe. Get him to shut that silly bastard Ade up. He's the only one who can handle him when he's drunk.'

Trev sped off like an arrow from a bow. Sonia took Philippa's hand and held it tight. She was a love.

'I'd shoot the lot of them,' said Brian.

'Don't talk like that, Brian. The Kikuyu are nice, most of them. They're more scared of the Mau Mau than we were.'

'I know,' said Brian, glooming out over the Broad. 'But it makes you want to *do* something.'

She thought again how Anglo-Saxon he was. Start a war, biff, bang, wallop. Settle it one way or the other; winner takes the lot. Nothing complicated. And yet ten to one he'd never seen anything dead that was bigger or more important than a pet cat run over by a lorry. He'd probably *cry* over a dead cat.

'Here's somebody coming,' said Sonia.

Three men; a tall one, not very steady on his feet, between two small ones. Ade Tshombe walking, staggering, between Trev and Sam Otenbe, and even in that dim

70

light their escorting faces, black and white, were as solemn and set as executioners!

'My friend wishes to apologize,' said Sam Otenbe severely. 'He knows he has been talking through his damned hat. He is drunk as usual, the black bastard. When he has apologized, I will take him home to bed.'

Ade Tshombe and Philippa looked at one another. She caught again that same old uneasy rolling of the eyes, in the dark face; smelt the same old fear on the black skin. God, how they must loathe us inside, she thought. Stealing their countries from them, swaggering about like pale-skinned gods. . . .

'I'm sorry, missus,' said Ade Tshombe. 'I'm sorry to hear about your troubles. I didn't think. I'm not from them parts of Africa. We don't have that kind of thing in Nigeria.'

He said it like a child coached for a school play; like a parrot. It was not his thoughts; it was what Sam Otenbe had told him to say. You'd like to hit me, really, she thought wildly. You'd like to rape me. And if you did, I wouldn't blame you. Not after what I've done to black people . . . .

But she made herself tell her lies in return.

'I know you didn't mean it. You weren't to know.' Then, screwing her courage up to screaming pitch, she held out her hand to him. He took it; his hand was soft and damp and sweating. She just wished he'd go away and leave her in peace. Her head was starting to throb.

'Goodnight, missus.' He was pulled away, quite savagely, by Sam Otenbe. But then he turned back, and said,

'I'm truly sorry.'

And that time she rather thought he was.

And then she leaned on the rail of the jetty, and looked

down at the swirling dark water, and thought it was full of dead faces.

'Get some more drinks, Trev,' said Brian, letting out his breath with a whoosh. Then Trev was gone, and Sonia with him to help him carry the glasses.

'You know . . .' said Brian, and she tensed herself against what was coming, some student profundity about race that would make her want to scream afresh.

'You know,' he repeated, 'boats coming up to this jetty sometimes go aground just out there. You know what on? Beer-glasses. We used to hold beer-glass throwing competitions out here, but the landlord didn't like it, so he stopped it.' He sounded so *affronted* that she suddenly burst out laughing; and felt a lot better.

'Oh, Brian, what would I do without you?'

'I'll bet you say that to all the men.' But he squeezed her tight in an enormous bear-hug, and tilted back her face and kissed her. And she just let him. She hadn't the strength left to refuse, even if she'd wanted to. But she didn't even want to. He smelt of English sweat and English beer, and it was a good cure for dead faces.

Chapter Eight

They gathered in the Shed, soon after eleven, a motley piratical crew. Even Trev was affecting a neatly-rolled black balaclava round his small skull. Terry, of all people, was sporting a big black clerical wideawake with a floppy brim, as well as a college scarf in lurid green and purple, both of which items the girls immediately stole from him. Terry's pretty pale, depressed-looking clerical girl-friend even showed a flash of angry eyes for once, grasping that tonight, not even Terry was to be considered safe. . . .

Philippa looked at these Cambridge mathematicians, these sturdy Sheffield civil engineers, and sophisticated female linguists back from their year in Paris, and thought they looked like . . . children waiting for Santa Claus.

Her own head was still throbbing gently. Four half-pints of cider, over the evening, had kept the headache quiet, but at the same time seemed to have fed it, so that it might leap on her and devour her at any moment. She almost decided to go to bed; which would have saved a lot of grief, as she was to realize bitterly later. But . . . it seemed so *old* to go to bed, and let the children go off and have adventures. She might be a murderess but tonight, she wanted a little adventure too.

Once outside, she could see why they sometimes failed to find the mill at all. It was said to be down a network of dark winding country lanes towards Potter Heigham. Half the assembled company, being new to harvest camp, hadn't a clue where it was. The others, having merely followed the leader the last time, were little better off. Only Brian had any confidence that he could find it, and Brian was at least half-drunk. He was the sort that turned merry with it. His voice never seemed to stop, but far from slurring, it became exceptionally smooth and clear. He said it had a life of its own when he was in this state; he could sit back and listen to himself talking, and was quite amazed at the wit of some of the things he said.

Besides which, nobody had a front light for their bike. Two had rear-lights that worked, and it was arranged that they cycle at the back. For the rest, Brian had obtained a lighted hurricane lamp, which he hung from his handlebars with a lordly air, saying the police couldn't touch them now.

It was not as dangerous as it seemed. The roads of Norfolk then were emptyish, even by daylight. At this hour, farm people would be safe tucked up in bed, and there were no commuters from London within seventy-five miles, and their tradition of fast driving after midnight was still thirty years away in time. The flock of bicycles moved very slowly, and if people fell off, they fell off with the dreamy slow-motion of drunks, laughing into a hay-filled ditch. Then there'd be a flutter of laughter through the flock, and more people would fall off from laughing. The main concern was that the large bottles of cider weren't broken.

They seemed to travel endlessly between the dark high hedges, trailing their good humour with them. Everything centred on Brian; everybody called out to Brian, Brian was the king, and on his cross-bar, she was the queen. It was very, very comfortable, after her long, long loneliness.

Slowly, the conviction grew on the party that Brian was not going to find it tonight. Slowly the conviction grew that he would not even be able to find his way home again. It only made the adventure more deliciously absurd. The night was warm and the air past their bare arms and legs balmy. A full moon appeared, and flirted with broken clouds. And yet there was a thread of seriousness about them, like pilgrims. There was no thought of having a picnic anywhere but at the haunted mill. If they didn't find it, the bottle of cider and tins of cake would be put away for another attempt another night. Philippa wondered how, in the mists of time that covered eight years of harvest camps, the tradition had started. A freak adventure of one or two, slowly growing to a tradition comprising the whole camp; except two. And even those two, bitter, angry, excluded, just made the present moment closer and warmer and comfier.

'Hey, Brian, did you know we just passed Norwich Cathedral?'

'That was the railway station at North Walsham . . .'

'Is that damp patch on your trousers blood or cider?'

'Blood, thank God.'

And then Brian said in a loud dramatic voice, 'I can sense it. We're near. This crossroads is definitely on the way there! I've passed it before.'

'You've passed it three times tonight already!'

The laughter brought them to the verge of a mass pile-up. Front wheels wobbled violently, and nailed shoes scraped on the road.

But Brian turned violently left, and shouted, 'Come on, come on, it's *calling* to me.'

'That's the ferry-keeper's wife at Great Yarmouth!'

'It's so close, so *close!*'

'There's rain forecast, too!'

A sharp swerve to the right, and then a massive presence lowering over the hedge.

'There, you bastards,' shouted Brian in glee. 'I *knew.*'

They were all suddenly very busy; the men breaking down the great banks of nettles for the girls. The girls screaming that they'd still been stung, and the men shouting, 'Whereabouts?'

The mill door was chained; Brian said it was always chained. There was a roughly lettered notice saying the mill was a dangerous structure, but the notice had fallen off and was rotting among the nettles. Brian pulled down two planks that had been nailed across a small window, in a lordly sort of way, saying they always shoved them back afterwards; and got over the sill. There were long sharp shards of dirty dark glass, still embedded in the sill and Brian reached back and grabbed Philippa round the waist and behind the knees, and lifted her through bodily, to a roar of appreciation from the men. To be handled in such a proprietorial manner was alarmingly pleasant.

Then they were tiptoeing up the flights of curving wooden stairs, Brian testing each one as he went and pronouncing it still safe, though many creaked loudly under his considerable weight.

They stopped about half-way up. 'We always make camp here; the floorboards are rotten higher up.' They sat down against the wall, and the rest filed past them, arranging themselves in a solemn circle, as if it was a committee meeting or a religious ceremony. Some of the smaller, lighter people went one floor higher, and peered down through trapdoors and holes in the floorboards. Philippa glanced around. There was surprisingly little to see. The central drive-shaft of the old mill, that transferred the power from the long-gone sails to the machinery below, ran up the centre of the circular room, from floor to ceiling; adzed roughly into an octagonal section. There was a sprinkling of dried mouse-dirt, like tiny dark grains of sand, that had drifted to heaps an inch thick in the corners; and a rusty lid from a paint-tin, full of dark blobs that Brian said was rat-poison. Beyond that, only the boarded walls, with whitewash flaking off them, and the loose flakes whirling like dervishes on the ends of short cobwebs, in the new draught from the broken-open window downstairs. And other small windows, letting in pitch-dark night to the glowing golden circle of the hurricane lamp.

To have come so far, with such struggle, for so little!

But then she saw the rough letters scratched into the whitewashed wood.

MIKE OXFORD 1949–52

JOAN CHELTENHAM LADIES 1941–48

And a great lopsided curving heart drawn round the two names, and a stringy arrow drawn through the heart.

On and on her eyes went, from name to name, date to date, heart to heart.

'There's mine,' said a man, pointing with great satisfaction, 'from two years ago.'

'And who was *she*, then?' asked the girl with him.

'Rita? She was reading chemistry at Reading. She was nice.'

'Nicer than me?'

'Don't know yet. Tell you later.'

A furious punch and wrestle started.

'I see you've seen the writing on the wall,' said Brian.

Philippa smiled at him. 'Just like one of your churches. Memorials to dead romance.'

'I tell you,' he said solemnly. 'I met a bloke here once, with his wife and two kids. In daylight, of course. Lecturer at Corpus. Brought his wife back to see his name, scratched on the wall in 1946. The girl's name inside the heart with his wasn't even his wife's either. His wife looked very fed up.'

'Don't blame her.'

'Can I scratch your name on the wall?'

'Depends if you're good . . .'

'Good at what?'

But she couldn't say no to him; not to the king happy in his kingdom. . . .

At that point, there came an interruption. A low rumble far to the north, across Hickling Broad.

'American night-fighters . . . ?'

'Tunder,' said Trev, getting up to look out of the small broken window. 'A dry tunder-storm, I think. I saw a flash.'

A thunderstorm in their ordinary lives might have worried them. But not on this magic night . . . when even getting soaked to the skin would be a laugh.

'Just right for a ghost-story,' said one of the girls, passing the cake-tin round comfortably.

'Ghost-story, ghost-story, ghost-story.' They banged on the floorboards with their feet and the heels of their hands.

'Trev!' said Brian. As the Anglo-Saxon king might have called on the favourite skald to sing a saga.

Trev got up, and took his rolled balaclava off. Then settled it more firmly down on his ears, as if about to set off on some perilous expedition. There was a silence, and an expectant wriggling of bottoms, as the girls moved into the protective circles of the men's arms and legs, firmly clutching their beakers of cider.

There was another rumble of thunder, much nearer, and one girl screamed, comfortably.

'I'd like to thank the Good Lord for his excellent sound-effects,' said Trev and got another laugh. Philippa watching his face, felt Brian's arms closed round her, tight, possessive. There was no harm in it, everyone was doing it . . .

Trev had changed. His Irish brogue was much more noticeable. His blue eyes had lost their scientific, cynical glint, and were large and saw nothing, except perhaps what was outside the mill, or inside himself. He waited, till the last wriggle and giggle had subsided. Philippa was reminded of Sir John Barbirolli, waiting to conduct Beethoven's Fifth. Here was a master craftsman . . . 'A bit less light, Trev?' asked Brian - cheekily nodding at the solitary lamp, and getting a last snigger.

'Turn it down just a touch, Brian,' said Trev with authority. He was the master now.

'I'm reminded of something that once happened to my Uncle Sean, down in County Kerry, when he was a very little lad, no higher than this. He was sent to stay with some cousins, who he didn't know at all well, and he was put in a room they called the Blue Room, though the wallpaper was bright pink, with roses . . .'

They listened to stories that seemed to flow one into another. Stories full of blue rooms, and long-lost doors discovered behind wardrobes, and the ghosts of nuns. And white cats met on the road home, which were the harbingers of death, and black dogs that were much worse. They did not seem like stories read in books. Everything had happened to some relative of Trev's; at times, he smiled, as if at a memory; at times, his face seemed to show real sorrow. The cake-tins and bottles of cider lay forgotten.

'There was once a poor young married lady, whose husband took her to live in a great dark house just south of Dublin. There she was alone all day, with only the company of two dogs, a brown one, and a black one. And they would wait behind her, in the mornings, while she put on her hat in the great dark mirror of the hall-stand, before taking them for a walk. And one morning, as she was putting on her hat, she heard the sound of a dog's feet padding down the stairs behind her, and she looked at the stairs through the mirror, and sure to God, there was no dog coming down the stairs at all, but only her own two dogs cowering and trembling at her feet . . .'

Outside the thunder rattled again, shockingly close, but still no rain. Philippa snuggled herself deeper against Brian, a Brian who was just warmth now and shelter, a breathing body and a beating heart against her back, in the starkness of the scrawled names on the whitewashed wall of the mill and the tiny flickering flame that was their only defence against the dark.

Trev was coming to the end of his tale.

'The dogs were so scared now they never left her side. Before bedtime, they would hide under the skirts of her bed, and then when she put the light out, they would crawl into bed with her, for comfort, shivering. And there came a time when she couldn't stand them because, afraid as she was, they were *more* scared. So she fastened them up, that last night, in the cupboard under the stairs, so she could try and get some sleep. And she'd just put the light out, when she heard a dog's paws, coming along the corridor lino, and the dog jumped into her bed and burrowed close in the dark, slavering and shivering. And in a great rage she picked it up, thinking it had escaped from the cupboard and carried it back to lock it up again.

'And when she reached that cupboard door, she was puzzled to see it was still fastened. But she flung it open.

'And there they were still inside the cupboard, her own two dogs, the brown one and the black one, cowering and slavering . . .

'But there was still *something* cowering and slavering, in her own arms. . . .'

Trev sat down abruptly, as if he was somebody different altogether, and nothing to do with the stories; and buried his face in somebody else's beaker of cider.

There was a long silence, and then Brian said, looking at his watch, 'Crikey, it's three o'clock. Doesn't time go fast, when you're enjoying yourself?'

Then everyone was on their feet, clearing up the cake-tins, and yattering their heads off. Nobody looked at the small figure of Trev, now shrunk back again to even smaller than his normal size.

'Mind that fifth stair, it's loose,' said Brian, holding the hurricane lamp high.

'Do you think Trev really believes those stories he tells?' asked Philippa, lazily, as they wended their way homeward.

'He frightens himself silly with them,' said Brian, over her head. 'Once he starts, they seem to take him over and he can't stop. He'll be like death warmed up tomorrow. But it's all right, it's Sunday.'

'Does he always tell the stories?'

'Him or some other Irishman. It's dead dull at harvest camp without a couple of Irishmen.'

'There's one I can do without.'

'Mick? He's not really Irish. His father's a German

businessman in Dublin. He was interned during the war on the Isle of Man. Probably a Nazi. That's why Mick works so hard at being Irish. Anyway, shurrup about Mick. The night is yet young, and I'm enjoying myself.'

Other couples on bikes were starting to pass them. The clouds of the thunderstorm had departed, leaving the land as dry as before. A dry storm, as Trev had guessed. The moon was out and full, close to the horizon now, giving plenty of light to see by. And they were back near enough to the camp for the signposts to make sense. Brian's leadership was over, which was probably just as well. He was wobbling more, and pedalling slower and slower. There had been some finishing up of the cider, to save carrying the bottles home.

Somehow, she saw their fall into the ditch coming, as you might see an avalanche start, or a great tree start to fall. But her body didn't seem to mind, and her mind was too far off to do more than watch. The ditch was wide and soft, and they seemed to drift down into it, without fear and without pain, like two feathers from a passing bird.

As they lay sprawled, Trev wobbled past. He raised his right hand, like a Catholic priest, and said:

'Bless you, my children.'

Then he was gone, and the last of the straggled bikes with him.

Chapter Nine

They lay where they had fallen, listening to the last cries of the other riders, as they dwindled off into the night. There didn't seem any point in moving. It was immensely restful.

'There's the Plough,' said Brian dreamily, 'and the Pole Star. The Plough is also called the Great Bear, and the Americans call it the Big Dipper. Americans have got no souls . . .'

'*Where's* the Plough?' Even as a child she'd been no good at the stars. It all just looked one great wheeling trackless mass to her.

'C'mere and I'll show you.' She wriggled her shoulders and bottom towards him, till she lay comfortably with her head in his armpit. His large arm, with pointing finger, waved across the sky. Finally, she said she could make out the Plough, even though she couldn't. It didn't matter. . . .

'I can see the moon,' said Brian. 'Upside down. Caught in the branches of a tree. Big and fat and golden. The harvest moon, I suppose. My father always talks about harvest moons.'

She craned her head backwards, and saw what he saw. It did seem very strange, the moon upside down, caught in a tree. She got the idea she was hanging upside down, and the stars and black space were below her, not above. But she was quite safe, because Brian's arm was round her.

'S'incredible, this. Half-past three in the morning. I've never been outdoors at half-past three before. You've got the whole world to yourself, because nobody else wants it. And I always waste it by snoring away in bed. Doesn't bear thinking about. We might see fox-cubs playing, or badgers or *anything*.'

'Mmmm.' She didn't want to say anything else. She just wanted to go on swinging through space, back pressed safe to the curving earth and neck against Brian. Everything seemed to belong together. Nothing was fighting anything else.

Brian's arm hauled her a bit closer. His chest rose and fell. He breathed slower than she did. Odd. But nice. His hand squeezed her ribs. His fingers began counting them, under her shirt. But there was nothing frightening, or knowing about his fingers. They weren't men's fingers; they were a child's fingers. Yet she was flattered, that he should be curious about her ribs. Nobody had ever given them a thought before. Certainly not Max.

'Ribs are funny things,' said Brian. 'I count my own, when I'm in bed, falling asleep. Mine are much thicker than yours. It would worry me, to have ribs as thin as yours.'

She giggled. 'I manage . . .'

'*You* never end up at the bottom of a rugby scrum. I've heard mine *creak* . . .'

She felt his, suddenly curious. They were much thicker than hers. Massive. They reminded her of the ribs of prehistoric beasts, in the Science Museum.

'Ey, gerroff. That tickles.' He grabbed her hand tight, imprisoning it. She decided she liked being his prisoner. She said, 'Mercy, mercy, fair sir!' looking him in the face. Their faces were only about four inches apart. His looked different, mysterious in the moonlight. The face of a friendly, comfy stranger, his mouth slightly open.

Suddenly he kissed her. He kept his lips tight together and so did she. It was a child's kiss, notable only for its pressure, which made her teeth ache slightly. He hadn't a *clue*. But she must not say so; she must not hurt his dignity. So she said nothing, just let her head fall back on his shoulder.

Then he tightened his arm round her shoulders and hugged her. And she was reminded of a child hugging a favourite teddy-bear. Then he stroked her hair; and he might have been stroking a dog.

It was all so different from Max. No striving, no pretending, no *submitting*. It might have been some totally different activity.

But suddenly she knew it *wasn't*. The pit yawned at her very feet. She was about to be discovered. And inside her, just below the thin skin of lazy well-being, there was a wasteland. The dust-devils blowing in the mission yard, the dead face. She *must* keep Brian from stumbling into that mission yard . . .

She sat up abruptly, smashing the magic. The phrase flew to her lips unwittingly.

'Nearly four. We can't go on lying here. I'm an old married woman . . .' She patted her hair down, picked a piece of hay out of it.

'Married woman?' From the horror in Brian's voice, from the way his body clenched up defensively, she might have said 'Vampire'. His outrage came at her like a blow, so she said, without thinking, wanting to defend her good name,

'Well, a widow, actually.'

'*Widow*?' His voice, from being accusatory, became incredulous.

85

'My husband . . . died . . . out in Africa. That's why I came home. To get over it.'

His voice went respectful again, but small and incredibly remote. Careful; awed. Like all the other voices, everywhere she went. Making her feel like a small blackened Victorian church she knew, no longer wanted, dying of respectful neglect. She knew things would never be the same between them. Her holiday as a normal human being was over. She might as well pack up and go home.

'That must have been very awful for you,' he said. Picking his words with extreme care, so that every ounce of nourishment was filtered out of them. She wanted to grab his hand, insisting she was the same Philippa as a moment ago. That she still wanted to be held and stroked and kissed.

But she knew it was quite impossible. Those were not things that widows did. Widows must grieve, wear black, take flowers to cemeteries, think sad thoughts.

'We must get you back,' he said, getting up. As if she was some invalid, or undetonated bomb.

She rode back on his cross-bar, though she thought he would rather have walked beside her at a safe distance, wheeling his bike. He was careful not to let his thighs brush against her, or his chin touch her head. When he said goodnight, his hand went up, to his forehead, as if to raise some invisible hat he was not even wearing.

Blindly she stumbled away, up the line of women's tents.

The tents were all dark and silent. She and Brian had lain watching the moon a long time. But there was still a dim glow lighting up the walls of the last tent; hers. Christ, was Brod still awake, lying in ambush in her bed, mind full of sarcastic hating remarks? She couldn't stand it if Brod was still awake. She just wanted to bury herself in her bed, pull the bedclothes over her head, flee the coming dawn. She looked towards the tent, her ears listening for the least clue of a sound.

She just couldn't believe what she was hearing, when she heard the man's voice. Followed by Brod's giggle. Followed by a creaking of bedsprings from the old iron army bed. The man's voice came again.

'Just ease your bottom up a bit, can't you?'

The voice was Mick Schneider's.

But that was not the worst thing.

The dim hurricane lamp hanging from the tent pole outlined Brod's bed by the door, shadowed against the thin glowing canvas.

Brod's bed was flat and empty.

They must be making love in *her* bed.

Her first feeling was of blind rage. She felt like rushing in and belting them, screaming at them.

Then she realised that would be *exactly* what they wanted. And they would just lie there and mock her and the more she raged, the more they would mock. And the whole line of women's tents would be roused, and everyone would see her defeat. It would be the talk of the whole camp for days.

Oh, Mick and Brod wouldn't be *approved* of. But everyone knew some students did it sometimes. It wasn't the end of the world, particularly on a Saturday night . . . and how petty to make a screaming row over it. What was a *bed*? All the beds belonged to the harvest camp anyway. Everybody was here today and gone tomorrow. And though the vast body of students did not sleep with each other, they would die to defend other students' right to do so. Free love was vehemently propounded in college debates, by people who would never dream of actually doing it. Such propositions always won by a huge majority. Anyone defending Christian morality was a target for endless abuse, even by students who actually went to church.

She mustn't make a fuss, or she wouldn't have a friend in the camp. So she stole silently away, terrified now that they would hear her, and call jeeringly after her.

And, at that moment, as if the very gods were against her, it began to rain. Big heavy drops. She thought of going to Sonia's tent. But Sonia would be asleep, and she wasn't quite sure which tent Sonia was in, the fourth or the fifth in the row. If she tried to find her, she'd rouse the camp.

She ran to the Shed, through the downpour. But the Shed was locked, and the rain was driving in under the verandah. There was no shelter there.

The cookshed was locked too, to stop people nipping in to nick grub in the middle of the night. By the time she'd futilely rattled the handle, she was half-soaked.

That only left the toilets and the wash tent. The smell in the toilets was unthinkable, so she slipped into the wash tent. There was little shelter there, either. The rain was drumming heavily and the canvas roof was already leaking in several places. And the rain was coming in through the unglazed windows, and seeping soggily through the trampled grass from the tent walls.

She moved two enamel bowls with a loud clatter in the dark, and sat on one of the tables, hunched, hugging herself with even colder hands. She tried to snuggle deeper inside herself, a trick she had learnt since Max died. But the cold and wet and dark and loneliness followed her inside. She began to shiver, uncontrollably. It must be shock . . .

She tried to rally herself. You're a grown woman,

twenty-four years old . . . training to be a doctor, for God's sake . . . you're not a child . . . you've survived far worse than this.

That was a mistake. The far worse came to haunt her, too. All the defences she had put up in the last two months just crumbled away. She might never have left that mission station.

In the depths of her despair, moving her head restlessly, she looked out of the gaping window.

Along the line of men's tents, there was a dim light. In one tent there were still people awake; light, dryness, warmth, human contact.

She knew who it was, who must be awake. It could only be Brian and Trev; the great talkers. And something told her that was the tent she *mustn't* go to. That light was a temptation, a diabolical temptation. She couldn't quite understand why . . . they would only be kind. But somehow she knew she mustn't. She held out for a full ten minutes; then a fresh drip of water from the leaking roof trickling down her neck cracked what control she had left. She would *not* be tormented like this; there *must* be help.

Sobbing and gasping in the downpour, she ran towards the light.

Even then, she halted at the door of the tent. There was a murmur of contented voices; Brian's and Trev's. She heard Brian say:

'I like being in a tent on a night like this. The rain only makes it cosier.'

'Provided your roof doesn't leak.' Trev seemed to have recovered his sardonic view of life.

She mustn't go in. She mustn't break their peace . . . then she heard Trev say:

'I think I heard somebody outside . . .' And Brian,

'Not that bloody Mick, for God's sake ... Even he wouldn't be so mad on a night like this ...'

'Fine night for loosening guy-ropes and settling quarrels ...'

Trev's head looked out of a small gap in the flap, cautiously.

'Philippa! What you doin' here, for God's sake? Come in, girl, come in.' And he undid the toggles, and pulled her in.

She sat on the bottom of Trev's bed, and dripped onto the duckboards. They had given her a fag, but her wet hands had put it out.

'It's insufferable,' said Brian. 'He's doing it to get back at me, you know.'

'How d'you make that out?' asked Trev.

'She's my woman, isn't she? If I can't take care of my woman ...'

Philippa wanted to say 'I'm not *your* woman. I'm my own woman.' But her teeth were chattering too hard.

'Let me go and talk to them,' said Trev. 'I can make them see reason. I can sort it out.'

'Like hell you will. That bloody Mick needs teaching a lesson. I'll shame him in front of the whole bloody camp. You see if I don't.'

Funny, he looked like a little boy in his blue striped pyjamas, with his blond hair rumpled. But he didn't *feel* like a little boy at all.

'Look,' said Trev, 'we can manage here till morning. You and I can share, and Philippa can have my bed.'

'And when someone sees her leaving in the morning?'

'All right, then. I'll get Terry up to deal with it. That's what he's paid for.'

'He's a bloody old woman. Useless. There's only one way of dealing with this.' Brian reached up and grabbed his old raincoat from a nail in the tent-pole. And the next second he was out barefoot into the rain.

They didn't catch up with him till he was nearly at her tent.

But then he paused, listening. They joined him; and listened to the noises coming out of the tent that had stopped him. They were familiar enough to her, as a married woman; she had faked them often enough. But to Brian she knew they must be new and baffling.

Chapter Ten

'Hey, Schneider, I want a word with you!' Brian's words came out in a demonic hiss.

There was no reply. The volume of sound within the tent was slowly mounting.

'Schneider, you bastard, do you hear me?' Brian's fury was mounting too.

She wanted to warn him that Mick couldn't hear him; that in the state Mick and Brod had reached, there was nothing in the world but two bodies. That Mick wouldn't hear an atom-bomb going off. But how to put it, quickly, so he could understand, out here in the dark and rain?

'Schneider. If you don't bloody come out I'll come in and get you!'

'Brian!' she faltered, reaching for his back.

'SCHNEIDER!' Brian's enormous roar echoed along the line of the tents; they must have heard him in Hickling village. There were sleepy querulous yelps from the other girls' tents. Flaps would be opening.

'SCHNEIDER! YOU BASTARD I'M COMING IN.' Brian's head went in through the flap. Before his body had time to follow, he was catapulted backwards by an enormous naked shape that leapt from the tent, flailing with both fists. Brian went down in a heap before him, a heap of tangled raincoat and pyjamas. The huge naked shape stamped on Brian as he lay there.

Somehow Brian got to his feet.

'For Christ's sake!' he got out, and then Mick knocked him flat again. Moved in to jump on him again.

Brian rolled away desperately among the tent-ropes. Which gave him a chance to get to his feet. His pyjama trousers had fallen down round his ankles.

Mick hit him smack in the mouth. The sound of the blow echoed down the row of tents, where a growing crowd of dim gaping figures was gathering.

'*Right,*' said Brian. It was a dreadful sound; it didn't sound like Brian at all. It sounded like the sound a wild animal might make, before it killed something. It must even have penetrated the wild fog of Mick's brain, because for a second he hesitated.

Brian threw down his raincoat. His pyjama jacket was flapping open; he was nearly as naked as Mick now. But some small part of Philippa's brain observed detachedly that there was nothing sexual in it. Both men seemed shrunk to nothing but a dark patch of pubic hair. They were . . . prehistoric was the only word she could think of. Or like something off a Greek vase of naked warriors. It had nothing to do with love, and everything to do with dreadful war. Virgil. *Bella horrida bella et Tiber spumantem sanguinem* or something, said a silly detached part of her mind.

Then Brian flung himself at Mick.

It could never have been fair. Mick was on his way down and Brian was on his way up. Mick was dazed, uncertain now. Perhaps he saw the crowd of girls watching . . . Brian could not have cared less who was watching. Brian did not mind being hurt, if only he could hurt in return. The two enormous shapes struggled and swayed in the dim light of the tent-lamp; huge slabs of muscles curving for a second in dim glowing arcs, then vanishing back into the darkness. Fists hit flesh with a wet solid slam. Panting and grunting and spitting. Mick was no coward, and it was obvious he was used to fighting. This wasn't two drunks flailing outside a pub that Philippa had once watched, first appalled and then with mirth, because both were so afraid of being hurt that they had flailed for ten minutes and neither had managed to touch each other at all. The only thing she could liken this to was two tom-cats she had once seen fighting on a coalhouse roof, locked into a turning, clawing, biting, screaming bundle while grey and orange fur blew from them like autumn leaves. Fighting about territory, without a she-cat in sight. . . .

It was too dark to see faces, and yet she saw the end coming. The further figure, in the midst of the welter of blows, seemed to begin to hunch, to shrink in on itself, almost as slowly as a dying plant. The blows of the other flailed into a crescendo. Then the nearest figure seemed to hurl both arms aloft, in a gesture of triumph, and the further one arced away from it in a staggering fall among the tent-ropes. There was a loud thud, and the falling figure lay still.

The figure still standing drew a hand across its nose, in a great bubbling breath, then looked at the back of its hand. Then it said to the fallen,

'Get up, you bastard.' The voice must have been Brian's. She still couldn't recognize it, but it certainly didn't have an Irish accent.

From the other figure came only a deep snore.

Just at that moment, the first of the men arrived from their tents, panting, demanding to know what the hell was going on. Among them, Terry, wearing his ridiculous clerical wideawake against the rain, and flapping his hands ineffectually.

He took one look at the two naked figures and said;

'Come on, chaps, play the game! There are ladies present.'

The menacing primitive figure of Brian seemed to deflate. Philippa saw him looking round desperately for his raincoat and pyjama trousers. She grabbed up the raincoat and gave it to him. The trousers must be somewhere under the feet of the encroaching girls.

Terry advanced, timidly. 'Who's that?' he asked the snoring figure on the ground. 'Mick, Mick! Come on, get up. There are ladies present. Mick! Mick! MICK!'

The tent flap opened, and Brod looked out. The cunning bitch, unlike Mick, was now fully-dressed. She took one look at the recumbent Mick and screamed like a steamwhistle.

'You've killed him, you've *killed* him.'

'She's hysterical,' said Terry, as if that solved everything though he made no move towards her.

That horrible screeching going on and on! The chance was too good to miss. Philippa stepped forward and slapped her hard across the face; that was what one did to people who were having hysterics; it was also immensely enjoyable. But it did not have the desired effect of silencing her. She came at Philippa still screaming, her hands clenched to talons. Terry, stepping in between, with belated gallantry, got his face thoroughly scratched and staggered back saying;

'Oh, I say!'

Terry's girlfriend, with quite un-Christian venom, laid hands on the still screaming, clawing Brod. So did Terry's girl-friend's best friend, a large blonde from a PE college. Brod immediately burst into tears.

'We were only having a cuddle,' she said, pathetically, 'and that fool attacked us. He's just not normal.'

'That's a *lie*,' shouted Philippa. 'You were making love. On my bed. And he was trying to stop you.'

It might have gone on a long time, if Trev hadn't said quietly; 'I think we'd better see to Mick. His breathing doesn't sound normal.'

It wasn't so much what he said. It was the way he said it. The still small voice of disaster.

Suddenly the men were around Mick; suddenly the men thought they knew what to do.

'Get him into the tent.'

'Get some blankets over him.'

'Strong sweet tea. Three sugars.'

As a medical student, Philippa knew they were doing it all wrong. She shouted at them, but they weren't listening. In a scrum, with what seemed hundreds of willing hands, they lifted the huge, wet, glistening body into the lamplit tent. Little droplets of rainwater, like dew, lay entangled in Mick's dark pubic hair, and his member was as tiny as a child's, a tiny wet white slug.

'I'll phone the doctor,' said Trev. 'From the callbox in the village.'

'Call an ambulance, too,' shouted Philippa. Then she pushed her way in through the scrum of men in the tent, shouting,

'Stand back, I'm a medic.'

The men fell back round the tent walls, telling each other to stand back, she was a medic. Some fool at the back was saying they should undo Mick's collar to give him air. Philippa shoved aside about eight blankets that had been

96

wildly piled up on Mick, and turned him on his side so he wouldn't choke on his own tongue. He was breathing very heavily. He was icy cold. His pulse was slow and faint. There was a nasty mess of hair and blood at the back of his left ear. There was little sign of a bump rising, and that was bad. His eyes were still tight shut. In the background, the same fool was babbling did anyone have any brandy? Someone told him to shut up, and an awful silence fell.

Suddenly, Mick's eyes fell open. They looked totally uncomprehending, clouded. Then they fastened on Terry, who was crouching next to Philippa. Mick's eyes seemed to clear. He flung out his arms towards Terry, and shouted, absurdly;

'Mam! Mam!'

The next moment, his whole gigantic body was in motion on the bed, aiming for the shrinking Terry.

'Hold him down,' yelled Philippa. 'Hold him down.'

A dozen willing hands reached out to comply; but Mick seemed to have acquired the strength of a maniac. He was nearly on his feet.

Another massive shape grabbed him and bore him back onto the bed. Brian. Brian back in the land of the living, pale and shocked but doing what was needed.

'He's got concussion,' he said. 'I've seen it playing rugger. They always think someone's their Mam.' He lay across the struggling Mick's chest, talking to him as gently as a mother. 'It's all right, Mick, mate. It's all right. You're safe. I've got you.'

'Mam,' said Mick once more. Then his eyelids dropped like curtains again.

'Concussion,' said the ambulance man, 'and maybe worse.

That could be a fractured skull. I hope not, for his sake. How'd he do it?'

'He fell, and I think he hit his head on a tent-peg,' said Brian, less than truthfully.

'And I suppose you did, too?' said the ambulance man, pointing at the far side of Brian's face, that Philippa had not yet seen. Brian turned his head to the light. His right eye was completely closed, and there was caked blood from his hairline to his jaw on that side. He looked so ghastly that Philippa had to bite her lip to stop from screaming.

'You'd better come with us in the ambulance,' said the ambulance-man. 'And will you come too, miss? You seem to know what you're doing.'

It seemed to Philippa a very ill-equipped ambulance. Mick lay on a stretcher on one side, and the three of them sat on the other. But there were no straps to hold Mick down. Every time the ambulance took a tight corner, it seemed to go up on two wheels and tried to catapult Mick onto the floor. They all had to make a concerted dive to stop him. And every bend in that Norfolk road was tight, and the driver was driving like a maniac, and trying at the same time to talk over his two-way radio to Casualty at the Norwich hospital. Casualty kept demanding details of pulse and respiration, and the driver kept yelling through the sliding door to his mate; and Casualty thought he was yelling at them, and yelled back, and his mate yelled at Philippa, and Philippa yelled back, and the mate yelled back to his driver who yelled back at Casualty, who yelled back again. And that damned sliding door kept slamming open and shut at every bend with a noise like a cannon going off.

The only silent one was Mick. His eyes were permanently shut now, his face in the blue light of the ambulance was like sweating marble, and his breathing was so shallow she had to strain to hear it. The only sign of life in him was that his eyelids flickered, and he kept on opening and closing his mouth, drawing out a longer and longer strand of saliva that bridged the gap between his upper lip and his lower. Philippa, in that dim blue light that made the ambulance seem so dark, watched that strand of saliva, fascinated. In some mysterious way, it seemed to her to represent Mick's life. If, on the next opening of Mick's mouth, it snapped, she was sure he would die.

And she would have caused *another* death. Was this her fate; to live on and be the cause of death in others? It seemed a fitting punishment for what she had done; a fitting lifelong revenge devised by Divine Justice . . .

She gave a quick glance sideways at the grotesque bloody mask of her other patient. Its expression was unreadable, but its mouth never ceased to talk gently to the unconscious Mick, telling him over and over he was going to be all right, that everything was going to be all right. Brian seemed to have no thought for himself; or for what he'd done; or for what was going to happen to him if Mick did die. The penny mustn't have dropped yet. He wasn't worrying about a manslaughter charge, only about his dear old mate and bosom friend Mick . . . she thought she would never understand the mystery of men as long as she lived.

They pulled up at Casualty at the hospital just as the big neon porch-lights were fading in the dawn. The ambulance-men and a gaggle of nurses bore Mick away from them on a trolley leaving Philippa's arms and chest feeling cold and empty, leaving her feeling she had been robbed.

She and Brian were shown to a row of tubular chairs with slashed seats, set against the usual green wall, which had initials carved into it. She thought wearily that Brian, the old Brian, might have said the wall was another memorial, another church full of memories. But the new Brian had nothing to say. He stared at his large but shapely bare feet, through his large and shapely clenched hands. He let himself be led away by a stiff large-bosomed staff nurse for his own treatment.

'You young men,' said the staff nurse with contempt. 'Saturday night is always the same, fighting and brawling, then coming to your betters to stitch you up. Don't you think of anyone but yourselves? Don't you think about your poor mothers? Don't you think about anything but drink?'

She stared at Brian's bare legs and feet as if they were the worst offence of all.

'I'm a student,' said Brian humbly, as if that was some kind of explanation. 'At harvest camp.'

'If I had my way, you'd all be put in a concentration camp.'

She brought him back after half an hour, looking a great deal more civilised. His face was clean; there was a neat row of big black stitches in his forehead, surrounded by a large yellow stain, and she had even found him a pair of washed-out blue hospital pyjamas and a pair of brown man's slippers that pinched his feet unmercifully.

'Students,' she said stiffly. 'If that's all they teach you at university, you might as well graduate straight to Borstal.'

Chapter Eleven

They sat on, a weary audience to the incomprehensible drama of the awakening hospital. The same characters swept time and again across the stage, meaninglessly. Flocks of chattering nursing orderlies, looking, with their arms enveloped completely in their brown cloaks, a little bit like plump starlings. The solitary technician, upright and proper in a buttoned white coat. A pair of young doctors, their tousled dress and hair a witness to their night's exertions, white coats open, shirt-collars open, stethoscopes dangling, inextricably mingled with ties, and heads close together over some deep matter. Nobody noticed Philippa and Brian; nobody spoke. Their necks began to ache with the continual expectant head-raising that never got an answer.

Only a sister came, for names and addresses.

'Mick Schneider,' said Philippa, then hesitated. Sister frowned. Of course Mick couldn't be his real name.

'Karl Gustav Schneider,' said Brian. '17 Brock Crescent, Dublin. His father's got an office in Dublin – Schneider Chemicals.' The sister looked surprised at this flood of accurate information, and asked hopefully,

'You don't happen to know his date of birth as well, do you?'

'Twelfth of August, 1930.' Then Brian added, 'How is Mick?'

101

'Still unconscious,' said the sister, and got up and left abruptly.

A first look of alarm crossed Brian's face. 'Still unconscious? That's serious, isn't it?'

'Maybe. Maybe not.' Philippa was anxious to take his mind off it. 'How did you know his name and address like that? And his birthday?'

'We used to be mates. We used to tease him about his name. We had a birthday party for him at the camp, two years ago. I used to write to him.'

'What happened between you two?'

'He got big-headed.'

She could have wept for him.

Soon after nine, a policeman in uniform came into the lobby, spoke to the receptionist, who nodded in their direction. She felt Brian tense up at the sight of the uniform.

The policeman came across, pulled out one chair of the row, and sat down facing them. He hitched up the knees of his trousers neatly, to stop them bagging, took out a notebook and turned the lobby into a police-station.

She knew she must speak first, because Brian was in a turmoil and might say anything.

'Good morning, sergeant!' She tried for professional crispness, and achieved it. The sergeant instinctively turned to her, as someone who knew what she was talking about, and they weighed each other up. This was no PC Plod. He was tall and thin, and very neat; his shirt collar was a little big for his neck, which gave him a cool well-laundered appearance. His hair was a rich red, and cut very short. His eyes were small and close together, but blue and very sharp. He looked like a fox, but a fairly amiable fox.

'Miss . . .?'

'Mrs . . . Philippa Moran.'

102

That put her one up, in the sergeant's book. But it also puzzled him. 'Are you . . . in charge of this . . . harvest camp, Madam?'

'No, only a student. I'm a widow. My husband died out in Africa, and I came back to continue my studies.'

He frowned a little, as if such an idea was not quite acceptable. 'Perhaps you will tell me your part in the episode. Take your time.'

She told her story, gauging the effect she was having by the sergeant's interruptions.

'A *midnight* picnic, in a *haunted* mill, Madam?'

'Just a student lark, sergeant.'

'I know about student larks, Madam. I was a student myself at Leicester for a year, but couldn't see the point of. going on. That's why my super sent me along.'

He did not seem to have enjoyed his year of student larks. He pushed on.

'Was the . . . injured man . . . on this student lark, Madam? No?'

'He thought it childish, and said so.'

'Was there much drink taken on this expedition? Only cider? . . . Had there been much drinking beforehand?

'Merry, but not drunk? Riding about on bicycles without lights in the middle of the night . . . a road traffic accident looking for a place to happen . . .

'You say you approached your tent, and heard the sounds of serious lovemaking? How could you be sure it was that, Madam?'

'I have been a married woman, sergeant.'

The sergeant blushed delicately.

'And you found this distressing, madam? As a married woman?'

'They were making love on my bed. I wanted to go to bed, and it was raining heavily outside.'

103

'And you were understandably distressed. What made you go to the acc . . . this young man's tent, madam?'

'His was the only one with a light still on. And he was the Camp Chairman . . .' Oh, Philippa, you are sailing close to the wind. What a strange thing is truth . . .

'He was *in charge of* the camp?'

'No – that was the camp organiser. He helped the camp organiser.'

'Why didn't you go straight to the camp organiser? Surely he was the one to sort this complaint out?'

'He was asleep.' The sergeant was not impressed. 'And he is a total weed. An ordinand – a vicar in training.'

A slight smile played round the sergeant's thin mouth. Then he said, 'Then you were expecting trouble, Madam? Trouble a weed wouldn't be able to sort out?'

She saw the trap. 'I was expecting a row. I wasn't expecting what happened.'

'Just so, Madam. So the acc . . . this young man accompanied you to your tent?'

'Yes, with another man.'

'The other man's name?' Oh, God, here was poor Trev being pulled into it. But she trusted Trev.

'Trevor O'Donnell. He was in Brian's tent. They were talking.'

'And what happened when you got to your tent?'

'Brian asked Mick to come outside, as he wanted a word with him. He called in through the tent door. But Mick didn't answer.'

'Why do you think that was, Madam?'

'Brian called very softly. He didn't want to wake the whole camp up . . . have everybody know what was going on. And it was raining very heavily. Noisily.'

'Understandable. What happened then?'

'Brian called again, louder. And still there was no reply. So he called louder still.'

'Loud enough to wake the other campers up?'

'Yes. I think so.'

'And then?'

'Brian put his *head* through the tent flap and shouted, and the next second, Mick leapt out stark naked, and knocked Brian flat. Without warning.'

'Why do you think that was, Madam?'

'I think he must have objected to being interrupted in . . . what he was *doing*.'

'I see, Madam.' The sergeant put his head down, but she saw his ears redden.

'Mick knocked Brian down twice, and jumped on him with both feet, before Brian began to defend himself.'

Oh, Philippa, where is the truth now? Brian *defending* himself? That terrible cry of 'Right'? That terrible shower of blows that had demolished Mick?

'And in the course of defending himself, he knocked this Mick down?'

'Yes, and Mick hit his head on a tent-peg . . .'

'Are you quite sure about that, Madam? It was dark . . .'

'Sorry. That's what people said must have happened. To cause that . . . place behind his ear . . .'

'Ah, yes, the place behind his ear . . . they think there may be a depressed fracture of the skull. They're having him x-rayed as soon as possible . . .' He turned to Brian.

'I must warn you, son, that this incident may give rise to a serious criminal charge . . . especially if the injured man should die. You are not obliged to say anything now. But I must ask you not to leave the district.'

Chapter Twelve

Once the sergeant had gone, Brian collapsed completely. Just sat with his head in his hands, as if he were never going to move or speak again. She became paralysed herself, by the size and inertia of him. Fourteen stone of tousled, helpless muscle, sitting in a filthy raincoat and pyjamas, in the lobby of a hospital that was getting more and more full of people who stared.

It was only discovering her purse, in the coat of her waterproof jacket, that got her into motion. Odd, that she had taken her purse to such a romp as the haunted mill; but she had been reluctant to leave it where Brod could find it. There was quite a lot of money in the purse, and in the money was the power to move Brian, which was all she could think about. She went to the reception desk, and put on her loftiest voice, her Establishment voice, to overcome her bedraggled appearance.

Huffily, and with a disparaging look, the receptionist phoned for a taxi. The taxi-driver, when he heard the destination, insisted on having the fare before he'd start the car. She had never been so humiliated in her life; but she supposed it served her right for playing at being a student.

In the back of the taxi, Brian groped for her hand, and held it very tight. She felt a little revolted, at such a mixture of physical strength and moral weakness. A frightened nine-year-old in the body of a giant wanting his Mum.

Through his other hand, still held over his face, came the bleats of a nine-year-old.

'Why did they have to bring the police into it? I've never been in trouble with the police in my life. I can't tell my parents. It'd bloody kill my mother . . .'

She stared out of the car window. It was the worst kind of Norfolk day. A dark grey sky over dark green leaves. The kind of day when you felt Norfolk was closing in on you, like a damp grey blanket.

'It's my parents I'm sorry for. They're law-abiding people. My mother hides in the loo if our chimney catches fire, for fear the neighbours will complain and the police come. I'm the only one they've got. They've sacrificed everything for me, and now I do this to them.'

She made herself give his hand a sympathetic squeeze. What had she ever seen in this pathetic heap?

'If Mick dies . . . if they send me to prison . . . that's the end of my college career. They won't take me back when I come out. I'll have to get some rotten little office job . . . but even *they* won't take a jailbird. What's going to become of me?'

She must make allowances. He was very young. He'd never been in trouble before. It was always the people who'd never been in trouble before who went to pieces when the police got their hands on them. Under that strain, even killers tried to commit suicide.

Well, I should know, shouldn't I?

She squeezed his hand again, and said, 'It might never happen, Brian. Mick might be conscious by this time. Sitting up and eating his breakfast . . .'

He caught at the hope with a desperate burst of enthusiasm.

'Yes, it'd take more than that to kill old Mick. He's as strong as a horse.'

She thought silently that horses could die too. She had seen them die. Big, strong horses.

'I mean,' said Brian, 'it was only a lark, a bit of fun really. Afterwards, we'd have shaken hands and been mates again. I don't hate Mick or anything. It's just that he gets on my wick sometimes.'

She went on squeezing his hand.

They got to the camp about midday. People were hanging round listlessly, waiting for lunch, and they gathered in a circle round the taxi.

'How is Mick?' asked Terry. He looked like he hadn't slept at all. He looked worried out of his mind. About what he was going to say to the NUS harvest-camp committee. Another chinless male wonder . . .

'Still unconscious,' she said, shortly.

'I keep phoning up the hospital,' Terry bleated, 'but they won't tell you anything. I mean, is it all going to blow over, or is it serious?'

'How do I know?' Men couldn't all be this bad, surely? Max hadn't been like this. Max would bow his head a moment, conversing with his God, then charge back into the fray like a hero. I could do with you now, Max, she thought, the first warm thought she had had about him since he died.

But it was a woman who charged in to the rescue now.

Sonia, her face pale and set, but strangely shining, came and took her by the arm.

'C'mon, I've got you a new tent; with me. You don't have to sleep with that bitch any more.'

And, suddenly weary to death, and with a last hopeless look at Brian, she let herself be led away.

The new tent was very close; beside the kitchen.

'This is a store-tent,' she said, dazed.

'I nagged Terry till he gave it to me. Let bloody Brod sleep with the spare shovels. The flap doesn't close properly on this one, but we'll manage . . .' Sonia put her arm round Philippa's shoulders. 'Look, I've got all your clothes and I've made your bed . . .'

'Bless you, Sonia.' Philippa felt an absurd desire to weep, because it all looked so cosy, like your bedroom at home when you were little, and your Mum could still make things better. It was very, very good to sit on the bed. She thought about nothing but the long ache of her back-muscles as they relaxed.

'I'll fetch you some hot water from the kitchen. In a bowl. Here's your soap and towel and things . . .'

She washed and changed and combed her hair in Sonia's little square mirror, hung on the tent-pole, and felt human again.

'The police have been,' said Sonia. 'It's serious, isn't it? They interviewed that hag, and she told them a pack of lies. We crept up to her tent and listened. God, you ought to have heard her. They were just having a little cuddle, her and Mick. Butter wouldn't melt in her mouth. I ask you, at three in the morning, and Mick starkers in front of the whole camp. Then she said Brian dived into the tent without warning and pulled Mick out and beat him up. She'll end up in prison for perjury, that one, if she doesn't watch it.'

Philippa's heart sank. 'Who else did they interview?'

'Trev. He was very steady. He told them the *truth*, and I think they believed him; and I said when I first saw Mick and Brian, Brian was on the ground and Mick was kicking him.'

'And did you?'

'Didn't see a thing. I was at the back. But that's what Trev said happened, and it's good enough for me . . .'

'Sonia! Now who's going to end up in prison for perjury?'

'You've got to stick up for your friends. What are friends for? After what that lying bitch said. She'd better not show her face round here again. D'you want something to eat? I can get you something. You don't have to come into the Shed, if you'd rather not . . . .'

'I think I just want to sleep, Sonia. Thanks all the same.'

Sleep was sweeping over her. She hadn't far to fall. She just lay down on the sun-warmed mattress, and was gone in an instant.

She wakened as it was getting dark. The hurricane lamp was lit, and burning low, so as not to disturb her. She felt dead: had no desire to move a muscle. All her muscles ached dreadfully, as if she'd done a killing day's work in the fields. She closed her eyes again, and just depended on her ears. The camp was very quiet. Far off, in the men's tents, one of the Basque students was playing his mouth-organ, very slow and sad. It all had the feeling of a battlefield, after the battle.

But nearby an argument was going on. A low-voiced loving argument. Sonia and Trev. Sonia concerned for Philippa and Trev concerned for Brian. Again, tears crept into her eyes, that there was still such love in the world. God bless the pair of them. She hoped they'd get married and have a lot of happy kids. But meanwhile, they were arguing softly.

'Look, I can't do anything with him. Philippa can cope with him, if anybody can.'

'She's worn out. It's not fair to expect it of her.'

'Look, he's threatening to give himself up to the police and confess everything. Says he might as well get it over with, and be in prison. Says he *wanted* to kill Mick. If he goes in this state they'll crucify him . . .'

Wearily, Philippa got off the bed and went to the tent flap.

They looked at her, their faces very close together, sitting on the grass in the dark.

'Now, you've *wakened* her,' said Sonia, crossly. But still lovingly. 'Can I get you something to eat now, Philippa?'

'Yes, please,' said Philippa. She wanted to talk to Trev.

Sonia ran off to the Shed, her long legs flashing in the lamplight.

'Any word from the hospital?'

'Terry's just come back. Went up there and pulled rank, and said he had to make a report to his headquarters. But when they told him the truth, I think he changed his mind about making a report. Mick's in a coma . . .'

'Oh, Christ!'

'It's bad, is it?'

'He could be in a coma for days, or weeks. Or years. Some people linger for years and never come out of it.'

'You better not tell Brian that, or he'll go right off his chump.'

'What's he doing at the moment?'

'Lying on his bed, doing a Sidney Carton act. "It is a far, far better thing that I do now than I have ever done." Sorry to seem so heartless, but he's being a bit ridiculous.'

111

'He's never faced anything like this before, Trev!'

'The trouble is, he's a *doer*. If he can't *do* anything about things, he goes mad.'

'I'll go and talk to him. Tell Sonia to bring the grub to your tent.'

She stooped to Brian's tent-flap. 'Can I come in?'

'I suppose so,' said Brian, in a dreary, hopeless voice. She wanted to kick him, but she just sat down on Trev's bed.

'What's all this tripe I hear? About you wanting to confess?'

'Might as well get it over with.'

'The police would like that, of course. Save them a lot of time proving you were guilty. Even if you aren't.'

'I *am* guilty. I felt like killing him.'

A kind of black, murderous rage filled her. 'You mean you wanted to see him in his coffin? You wanted to see him lowered into a hole in the ground? You wanted to see his face that would never move again, starting to turn into rotten meat?'

'God's sake . . .' He found the energy to sit upright, very suddenly. 'Not if you put it like that, no! I mean, it's his life . . .'

'Gracious of you to say so. So what end-result *did* you want? Be honest!'

'I wanted to flatten him. Knock him cold . . . I suppose.'

'Well you certainly managed that. And when he came round?'

'I wanted him to bugger off, I suppose. Or just shut up.'

'No permanent disablement? Broken legs? Brain injuries?'

'Of course not. He's got his degree to get. And he plays rugger for his college.' Brian sounded oddly indignant. Well, it was better than self-pity.

'So. You intended common assault. Not even grievous bodily harm. And under provocation . . . not exactly *murder*, is it?'

'I suppose not.' Now he sounded sulky, as if a toy had been taken away from him.

'You're nothing but a great big kid. Who can't wait for Santa Claus to come. Who knows, he might even bring you something *nice* . . .? You've got friends who care about you . . . you've got parents who care about you. Don't you think you owe it to them, to wait and see what happens?'

'Yes, Philippa.' He sounded utterly flattened.

'Have you had anything to eat?'

'No . . . I wasn't hungry. But I feel hungry now!' He sounded quite surprised.

'Well, you better share mine. Here's Sonia with enough to feed an army . . .'

And for a while there was a humble exhausted peace.

The following morning, Philippa felt better, just dazed and dozy. Trev managed to deliver a pale and shaky Brian to the Shed for breakfast. At least he was dressed for work. They sat, just the four of them, at a table in the corner. In the opposite corner, Brod sat at a table, alone, with a closed-up face.

'Nobody's talking to her,' said Sonia, triumphantly. 'They're saying she led Mick on, to spite you. There's a lot of sympathy for *you*, Philippa.'

'What about me?' said Brian, into his cornflakes.

'They say you were too rough. There's a lot of sympathy for Mick, too.'

'Anyone says anything to me, I'll *smash* them,' said Brian, venomously.

113

'That would really improve your chances,' said Trev, tartly.

At that point, Terry came wandering across.

'Brian, a word.' He glanced round nervously at the rest of the campers, and lowered his voice. 'Brian, I think the general feeling is that you ought to resign as Camp Chairman. I think you've . . . erm . . . lost the confidence of the campers. Only temporarily of course, purely temporary.'

'Right,' said Brian, his hands clenched, and there was an echo of the way he had said 'Right' before he hit Mick.

'And Brian . . . I don't think you'd better go out to work today . . . not in the fields . . . not till the feeling wears off. That'll be best, won't it?'

Please don't hit him, Brian, *please* don't hit him.

'Have I lost the confidence of the blackcurrants as well, then, Terry?'

Philippa could have hugged Brian, for that little spark of humour. But the next second, Terry was gone, and Brian had plunged back into his gloom and cornflakes.

Philippa, watching him, thought that on no account should he be left alone today. There was no knowing what state he would get into, what he might not do.

'Terry,' she called across the Shed. 'I shan't be going out into the fields either, today.'

Terry frowned, consulted his clip-board. 'We have to keep up our quota of workers, you know, Philippa. I can't spare you.'

'You know where you can stuff your quota, Terry,' she said, 'where it hurts most.' She was amazed by her own vulgarity.

The campers sniggered. The unpopular might wax and wane; but Terry was always among them.

114

The camp was silent, when the rest had gone. Behind the shed, you could hear the cook and the assistant cook rattling their washing-up, and that was all. Terry always vanished with his ecclesiastical girlfriend immediately after breakfast, in his pre-war Austin Seven. Opinion was that they went to church daily to pray for strength; that they had to, because their supply of it was so meagre.

She wondered if Brian was going to stay staring at his drying cornflake plate all day.

'Let's go and ring the hospital!' Anything to get Brian moving. They walked along to the callbox. It was a beautiful morning, not a cloud in the sky, all the birds singing their heads off. But it seemed just to add an extra twist to the screw.

Especially as the hospital reported 'No change'. Brian ended up staring at a tuft of roadside grass, instead of at his cornflake bowl. She *must* keep him moving; must give him something to do he was good at. Trev had been pretty shrewd there. She racked her brains.

'Let's go sailing. You promised to teach me to sail.'

Chapter Thirteen

Hickling boatyard was a delightful place, with each sailing dinghy lying in the water under its own little thatched roof on poles.

The old boatman remembered Brian from previous years. They put up the mast and sails together, with great chatter about do you remember old So-and-so who hit your jetty under full sail, yes, the tall thin one with the long black hair and moustache, the one who went around with the little red-haired girl, no, he's not here this year they say he's teaching out in Southern Rhodesia. No sailing dinghies for him to wreck out there, thank God harhar. She watched Brian trying to shake off his mood, get his confidence back, painfully trying to re-become the same good old Brian. Again, she could have wept for him.

Brian leapt into the dinghy at last, and held out his hand to her. The dinghy was rocking wildly, and looked very frail, like a highly-varnished eggshell lying in the dark water. But Brian's hand was firm, commanding. She sat down in the stern, and felt a little better; she had never been in a dinghy before in her life, and was alarmed to see more dark water sloshing around the duckboards under her sandalled feet. She was not a strong swimmer, and they said the Broads were full of long choking weeds . . . .

The old man gave the dinghy a strong and alarming

push with his foot, and the jetty floated away behind. Brian got out the oars and began to row through the smooth water under the trees, to where the surface of the Broad was broken by choppy little waves. He very much gave the impression of knowing what he was doing. In command. At least she felt pleased that her scheme was working. She felt a faint breeze in her face, watched with fascination as the hanging mainsail began to fill out with wind, like the belly of a pregnant woman.

'Mind your head! Duck!' Just in time, she ducked as the sail swept over, bringing the heavy wooden boom with it. Then it swung just as savagely back the other way.

'Stay down! I don't want to do somebody else in!' That was a very good shot at being the old Brian. He shipped the oars, and scrambled back to the stern, like a crab. Swung the tiller hard across. The sail steadied, the boat heeled over alarmingly, and a low, jolly, chuckling of water came from the bow and stern. She laughed, because it was both exciting and alarming, like the first time she had ridden a bike on her own, after her father had just let go of the bike saddle. She looked over the side. The dark murky water, full of paler weeds and tiny swimming creatures, seemed alarmingly close, swirling past only inches below the elbow of her jumper. She trailed her hand in it, tentatively, partly to show she felt at home, and partly trying to make friends with it, as if it was an inquisitive dog of uncertain temperament.

'Stand by to tack,' shouted Brian. 'When the sail goes over, jump to the seat on the other side. *And keep your head down*!'

Which involved a very undignified scramble, with her skirt all over the place, and then the boat heeling over even more dangerously the other way.

'Sit on the gunwale,' shouted Brian. 'Hang your bum over a bit. To balance her. But hang on tight or you'll fall in.' She hung on for grim death, her bottom only inches above the choppy waves, and feeling the occasional slap of dampness through her skirt. She did not think she was going to like this sailing lark much; there was a limit to what she would do, even to please Brian.

And then, quite suddenly, she got the hang of it. She watched for the sail coming over, and timed her leaps without having to be told. She began to enjoy hanging further and further out above the racing water. She began to understand what he was shouting about; how the little pennant at the top of the mast showed the direction of the wind, and how you had to match that with the angle of the sail, and the direction the boat was sailing. It was like that Triangle of Forces, learnt so long ago in Physics at school.

'Now you have a go steering her,' said Brian. And sat for a while with his large hand over hers on the tiller. Then he let go, and watched critically while she did it all for herself.

'Not bad. You're quick, for a girl.'

She sensed he had taught many girls to sail, the patronising young pup. But she didn't even try to kick him. The skimming across the green water, the widening ripples from the blunt bow, the sparkle of the waves in the morning sun, and the sparkle of the drops of water that came inboard and bedewed the varnished planks, even the dim blue trees on the far bank of the Broad far away, were all part of some glorious symphony. She felt *alive* as she hadn't done for years. And their bodies moved as one, now. It was like riding two-up on his bicycle, only better.

Brian's face, upturned to the little flag on top of the mast; his eyes picking up the blue of the sky and shining;

his mouth a little open with concentration, and his pink tongue poking out of the corner of it. He was *beautiful*. He was a good teacher; he'd be marvellous with kids. He'd make a marvellous father, because there was so much of the kid left in him.

He's much too beautiful to go to prison. If I have to lie my head off, she vowed to herself, I'll not let him go to prison. I'll not let them ruin him.

As if he had picked up her thought, he shouted.

'I couldn't bear not to be free. I couldn't bear to be locked up, with louts ordering me around, and being fastened in with *scum*. If Mick dies I shall run away. Vanish. Work as a farm labourer where nobody knows me . . .'

'Not *now*, please, Brian. Not while we're enjoying ourselves.'

He grinned at her and said, 'OK'.

Back and forwards they went, with her getting more and more slick with the tiller and the sail. A faint heat mist began to gather over the Broad; it seemed quite empty, not another boat in sight.

'The lot from the Pleasure Boat have gone,' said Brian. 'And the new boats coming from Potter Heigham haven't got here, yet. This is always the best time of day, here. Peace and quiet. It gets almost boring, sailing, once you're good at it . . .'

As if to undermine his confident words, there was a brattle of thunder, far off.

'Another of Trev's dry "tunder-storms",' he said, and laughed.

But as they tacked again, to start back up the Broad towards the Pleasure Boat, two miles away, he said:

'Jesus!'

She looked where he looked. The sky seemed to have

gone mad. Through the thick veil of mist, a towering mass of clouds was rearing up. The sun suddenly looked pale and cold, and then vanished.

'A squall,' he shouted. 'You sometimes get them with thunderstorms. Get some sail in, bloody quick.'

But as he stood up, the first gust of wind hit them. He sat down again beside her, with a thump that knocked half the breath out of his lungs.

'Too late.' He grabbed the tiller from her. 'We'll have to sail through it.'

So many things seemed to happen at once. The boat heeled over in a truly terrifying way, the bulging sail hitting the choppy water. A wave of dark water leapt across the dry gunwale to her feet, like a wild beast trying to eat her up.

'Lean out,' yelled Brian. 'For God's sake. As far as you can.'

Then the sail and boom came over with a terrifying crack, as if it was about to tear loose from the mast. And again. And again. And then they were running on a new course, with the gunwale just dipping every so often under the water, as if the dinghy was gently sipping a drink.

And then the rain, driving on the wind into her face, so she could hardly breathe. And crooked white trees of lightning, lancing down through the thick grey air, to the turmoil of the Broad, and the boat streaking along at terrifying speed, and she desperately trying to obey a string of orders as her hands and feet went numb with cold.

At one point, one of the small islands of the Broad, low and reed-laden, loomed up out of the flying water, just in front of them. They couldn't possibly miss it. They would overturn and . . .

She saw, in a dream, Brian bend forward and pull up

something in the bottom of the boat. Then they hit the island and went straight through it, slithering through the reeds like a sledge, and then down with a tremendous splash into the deep water on the far side.

'I pulled up the centre-board,' shouted Brian. 'That's a trick worth knowing.' And he laughed. Soaked to the skin, hair plastered down over his brow, he laughed. He was loving every moment of it.

If we die now, she thought, I shall always remember him laughing. And it did not seem so very terrible, to die now. It would solve a lot of problems. For him, and for her.

And then, with the perversity hidden at the heart of the universe, the squall began to die. Now, it was no more than wildly enjoyable; then merely sailing in a strong breeze. Then only a faint breeze. And then not a breath of wind at all. The rain had stopped too. Overhead, the sun came out strongly, back in its blue sky. But all around them, a thick warm mist lay on the water; water that slowly calmed until it was a smooth mirror; only broken by the plopping of small fish as they broke surface, livened up by the turmoil that had raged above them.

'What weather,' said Brian. 'Feast or famine! This bloody mist. Can you see land anywhere?'

He swung round, to look back over the stern. She could see every strong muscle of his body through his clinging transparent shirt. She herself felt naked in her wetness; naked and cold and damp and shy . . .

'There's a smudge over there that might be land,' he said. 'And what looks like an old mill or something.' He got out the oars and rowed towards it, and she watched the muscles of his body moving.

It was a mill; not the mill of the picnic, but a poor rotten wooden skeleton that reminded her somehow of a crucifix.

And there was no place to land; the dead reeds of last summer stood six feet high out of the water, silvery and damp, with this years' reeds climbing greenly through them. The only gaps between them were narrow black channels of mud and water, that had obviously been made by ducks.

They went on rowing hopefully, until they came to a little, half-sunken, wooden platform with green moss on it, and a wooden marker on a stick that said, crudely lettered, '34'. There was a sun-faded sodden packet that had once held Gold Flake cigarettes. And a rusty tobacco tin. And a grey, sodden, flat mat that had once been a *Daily Express*. Brian leaned over, making the dinghy tilt alarmingly, and picked it up.

'Six months old. This is a fisherman's place. Well, if fishermen can get to it, it must lead to dry land somewhere. Maybe we can find a pub and get a drink and dry off.'

He stepped ashore and tied the dinghy to a rotting stake, and then turned and lowered the sails. 'Don't want her running away and leaving us, if the wind comes back.' Then he gave her a hand and she squelched ashore.

But there was no pub. Nothing much, really. Just the skeleton of the mill, and some rusty machinery; cogs and gears, half-buried in the reeds, and some very doubtful-looking paths that meandered away into nothing after twenty yards.

And, in the shadow of the ruined mill, a small patch of ordinary green grass.

'No point to going on,' said Brian. 'You could get lost for days . . . We'd better wait here for a wind, and dry off.' And, without a thought, he stripped off his shirt and trousers and socks and sandals, leaving only his rather grubby underpants. He hung his wet things on the reeds, where they looked like absurd wet flags. Then he lay down full-length. 'We'll be dry soon. This sun's getting quite hot. I don't know about me wallet, though.' He began extracting things from it; photographs and pound notes: and spreading them out on the grass, as if they were some precious museum collection. 'I suppose Joe in the pub might take these notes when they're dry. He's a mate of mine.'

She shivered. The sun was getting hot on her bare legs, but the rest of her felt very damp and cold and profoundly uncomfortable.

'Why don't you get those wet things off?' said Brian. 'They'll dry much quicker on the reeds. And the sun will warm you up. I'll not look. I'll turn my eyes the other way.' And, good as his word, he rolled over, and went on fussing with the contents of his wallet.

She undressed reluctantly, watching the muscles of his bare back. She hung up her clothes on the reeds next to his, dressed only in her bra and pants. The sun was grateful on her bare skin, though she was still purple and blue in patches with cold, and kept running up into gooseflesh. Still, it was a lot more comfortable, naked.

She sat down on the grass, and felt . . . bored. The storm on the Broad had stirred her up, made her restless. There was nothing to look at but reeds, which totally cut off the view of the Broad. She heard the heavy chug of a cabin-cruiser's diesel, but it might have been in another world. She even felt tempted to go back to the landing-stage for that soggy newspaper, but she wasn't in a mood for reading either.

The view of Brian's back irritated her; made her feel, perversely, as if he didn't think she was *worth* looking at. He was far too busy fussing over his damned photographs and pound notes. And he was silent, probably starting to brood over Mick again. There was a dragon-fly hovering over his bare back, probably waiting to bite him. Dragon-flies had a nasty bite. She moved across to shoo it away. How beautiful his back was, deep brown with sunbathing, so that the little gold hairs on it showed up. She held up her hand, so that its shadow fell across the insect. It darted away instantly. *It* was aware of her. But Brian wasn't. He should have felt the touch of that cool shadow as well; but he gave no sign. Brooding for sure.

She said crossly, before she had time to think,

'I don't mind you looking at me. After all, you have seen me in my bathing-costume!'

'Bathing-costumes aren't sexy,' he said. 'When people bathe they get all cold and shrivelled up.' But he rolled over and looked at her. His eyes changed subtly, and she knew he liked what he saw. It warmed her. She had always used to think she had quite a reasonable figure; before she met Max. Max was above such things. She basked in Brian's approval and thought,

'I don't look like a grieving widow now.' She knew it was a wicked unworthy thought; *that* gave her a lot of pleasure.

But, lying on his back, Brian had closed his eyes again. The heat closed down on her; the heat and the silence between passing cabin-cruisers. She thought again that nobody must ever come here, apart from fishermen, and this was not the fishing season. The loneliness and silence were heavier and more languorous than the heat.

Brian seemed to have fallen asleep and she fell to studying him. She had never had the leisure to study a young male body before; Max had been a great one for pyjamas, even in the heat of Kenya. She studied the great slabs of smooth-skinned muscle, the tight places which shone

124

where bones poked up near the surface, the redundant looking nipples, like little crumpled prunes. She wondered what it was like, to be a man.

'Christ,' said Brian suddenly. 'I really can't put up with it.'

'What?'

She was startled to find he had been so still, yet not asleep.

'This bloody business with Mick. I keep on thinking it never really happened, and then I remember it did. It's like one of those animal-traps that poachers set, with steel jaws. Just waiting to fasten round my leg. I mean, if he recovers, it's *nothing* – just one of those things, shake hands and forget it. But, if he *dies* – they could put me in the nick for *years*. And what for? What good will it do them? What good will it do me? All that waiting to go on trial, and then everybody staring at me, and reading about me in the papers, and the neighbours talking. And then being left inside to rot. And then coming out all old and grey, with your life *finished*. What right have they got to do that to people? And all because some damned fool hammered in a tent-peg in the wrong place. I mean, all I did was to break up his clinch, like they taught us in boxing school . . . .'

'I don't know, Brian.'

'I mean, I've got to get my degree. Get a job. Get married. Have kids. What good will they do, shutting me up? I mean, I might discover something in chemistry . . . some cure for something. Isn't that more important than sewing prison mailbags?'

'Life's full of traps, Brian. I knew an old lady once . . . when she was eighteen, she went to Italy with her father, who was a landscape-painter. They rented a villa. He was out in the hills painting all day and she fell in love with the villa's young gardener. They made love, in the second week, and the boy was so scared he ran away and was never seen again. Frightened of what he'd done, I suppose. But she was pregnant. Her father didn't reject her – he blamed himself for leaving her alone all day – but he hid her away when they got home. She had a son . . . and he wasn't normal. Not an imbecile, but just not quite normal. She looked after him for sixty years, till the day she died. She had no other life at all. One week of joy and a lifetime of misery.'

'Jesus, you do try to cheer people up!' But at least he had opened his eyes and was really looking at her. And his eyes were outraged and shocked at what had happened to the old lady. Under all that surface chatter and bonhomie, he *was* sensitive. We all have to have shields against life, she thought, and his ever-chattering shield was a kinder one than most people used.

'I suppose,' he said slowly, 'you Christians would say she had been uplifted and purified by her life of suffering . . . sixty years of looking after someone can't be *pointless*.'

'She hated her son. She looked after him very well, but deep down she blamed him for what had happened to her. She hated most people. She just took a fancy to me.'

'Jesus. I feel *sick*. What an awful life. My Dad always says that every cloud has a silver lining. But that *was* just a trap. If I get out of this trap I'll make bloody sure I never get caught in another.'

'It's not that easy, Brian. If you could see it coming, it wouldn't be a trap. All you can do, once you're in, is to stay calm and not wear yourself out struggling pointlessly.'

His blue eyes, looking at her, were suddenly sharper.

'You're in some sort of trap, aren't you, Philippa?'

126

She clamped her mouth extra-tight, as if to stop her words getting out. But he said:

'I can tell. You keep so calm; you keep so still. Like an animal in a trap that daren't move in case it hurts itself more.'

'None of your business. It's all in the past now.'

'It was your marriage!' If he had sounded triumphant, her mouth would have stayed closed. But his eyes were full of the sort of compassion you have when you've just been badly hurt yourself. Of all the faces she had talked to since Max's death, only his was open. She would tell him a bit. Just enough to satisfy him. Then stop . . . .

She began pulling up stalks of grass, and making a tiny collection of them, in the palm of her hand. As if she was God, counting out souls.

'His name was Max – Max Moran. He was a medical missionary, a trained doctor. He came to our medical school, to talk about the work he was doing in Kenya. We had a branch of the Student Christian Movement and I was secretary being a vicar's daughter. I had to look after him during his stay, and show him round.

'He made it all sound so exciting, so real and vital. He wasn't the sort of Christian I was used to. Daddy was a very quiet, patient sort of Christian – thirty years in one parish had sort of worn him down – he did a lot of quiet good work, but he'd given up looking for big results. Max was different. Max was on fire for the Lord – in a hurry for his God. I suppose his certainty just swept me off my feet. I thought this is the big one, this is what I was *made* for. So I gave up medical school and married him, and went out to Africa because he convinced me that was what God wanted from me. Mummy and Daddy were very unhappy about it, but I just wouldn't listen to them. Max just filled my world. Looking back it seems like a madness.'

She looked up. Brian was watching her, intent, open-mouthed. Like a child. He looked very shocked, as a child would be, if one of its adults broke the rules of the game. She ducked her head down again.

'I suppose I felt guilty from the start. I'd left behind two very upset parents. But I thought I was doing God's work, and that in time God would soften their hearts and bring them round – that's what Max said would happen.

'But it wasn't just that. On the ship, Max insisted we spend hour after hour praying in our cabin. I'd always prayed a bit – but not like Max did, on and on, out loud. My knees used to hurt, and in the end I could think of nothing but my knees, and Max's voice going on and on till I could've *screamed*. I wanted to be outside in the sunshine, talking to the other passengers. But Max said they weren't real Christians, and that they were of no importance.'

She looked up again. The shock and horror were still on Brian's face. Shock and horror for *her*. If that look was still on his face at the end of her story . . . .

'And then, I began to have doubts. Max's God seemed to want exactly what Max himself wanted. Max wanted a son, in a hurry. So he became convinced that God *wanted* us to have a son. In a hurry. *My* feelings had nothing to do with it. My feelings were irrelevant. It was God's will. Always God's will.

'I think I began to hate Max then. So I felt even guiltier. If I was resenting Max, I was resenting God. Max said I was full of what he called "self-will". That was the worst thing of all, according to Max. Max made me confess my self-will. Not to God in private, but to Max, in public. There were two other missionaries on the boat, with us, an elderly couple I didn't like at all. Max used to hold prayer-sessions with them. He made me confess my self-will in front of them. Every day.'

'Hell,' said Brian. 'If he'd tried to do that to me, I'd have beaten him to a pulp.'

'Brian, will you *never* learn? Beating people isn't any sort of answer.'

So why was his answer like balm to her heart?

'When we got out to the mission station it was worse. The Mau Mau troubles were just starting. White people had been hacked to death on their farms. All the other whites were taking precautions, on the advice of the Army. Iron bars over their windows, heavy wooden doors with dead-bolts, ridgeback dogs, Masai watchmen, barbed wire . . . personal firearms. The Army had fortified the mission station while Max was away. Max was furious. He tried to make them take the window-bars away, but they refused. Max said Jesus wouldn't have had bars on his windows and dead-bolts on his doors, or dogs or guns. He said we had to live by *faith*. And if we were called upon by God to be martyrs, then it was our duty to let ourselves be killed. He said that the blood of martyrs was the treasure of the church.

'The other settlers were horrified for me. They tried to persuade him to take precautions; there were lots of arguments. But Max just laughed at them behind their backs, and said we were broadcasting the love and faith of God, even to the Mau Mau. I was absolutely terrified. Day and night, but especially at night, when Max was away.'

'The *bastard*,' said Brian. 'The rotten stinking *bastard*. Putting you through that.'

'One day, when Max was up-country, we had a detachment of soldiers camped nearby. The officer came to see me.

He was a bit like you. Not very old. Scared but brave, if you know what I mean. He was worried about me. I was very touched. He gave me this revolver. A Webley 45. He had one of his corporals show me how to aim and fire it. It was so enormous, I was nearly more scared of it than I was of the Mau Mau. When I fired it, even holding it with both hands, it nearly broke my wrists. But they insisted I keep it, loaded at all times. I had to hide it in a little ventilation hole, high up in the wall. Because I knew that Max looked through all my things when I wasn't there. Looking for evidence of what he called "back-sliding". If he'd found it, he'd have made me give it back to the Army. So I hid it, and it was a sort of comfort. Not that I thought I would ever use it, but because it was evidence that *somebody* cared about me . . . .'

She stopped. She simply couldn't go on any further. The pain was too great. She finished simply.

'So you see you aren't the only person who's ever been caught in a trap, Brian.' And looked up.

So many people had looked at her since Max died. The hard, tense, inquisitive faces of the police; the horrified faces of the Kenyan neighbours, the grieving, crushed faces of her parents, trying desperately hard not to say 'We told you so'. Much worse: the faces of Max's friends, who were determined to see Max as a martyr, a dead warrior for Christ, a near-saint. And her as a mere relic of the near-saint. They had talked of her going up and down the country, to their sick unhealthy meetings, telling the story of Max's martyrdom over and over . . . a whole prison made of faces, expectations. And none of them knowing the real truth that lay cowering within her.

But Brian's face was not at all like that. He had the same expression of waiting compassion as he had worn that morning so long ago, while he was waiting for the snail to cross the road.

Me and the snail; she nearly laughed out loud.

But he saw her face move to laughter, and he looked down, hurt. Oh, God, she couldn't bear for him to be hurt again; he'd been hurt *enough*. Her arms flew round him; she felt his warm breath between her breasts. And suddenly she couldn't get close *enough* to him. The smell of him, the feel of his skin under her lips was like food for the starving. Her body just took over; as her throat had, that morning in the pub. It became pure animal, and after the darkness of her mind, animal was beautiful.

He was nothing like Max; Max who'd been dominating, driving, always on top, and then suddenly nowhere, back turned, muttering to his God or snoring. Brian was like she was. Tentative, gentle, going on talking to her. They even laughed at times. Cosy. Friendly.

There were times when they rested, lay side by side. Times when she looked up at the gaunt, rotting mill, with the warped remnants of its four sails so like a crucifix.

Was it possible, barely possible, that God might not be like Max, but more like Brian? Somebody you could talk to? Laugh with?

But that could wait. For the moment, she lived content with sun and skin and smell and warmth, inside the circle of Brian's arms. To him, she was just herself, Philippa. Not Philippa Moran, but Philippa Stevenson, who had once been, and would be again. Somehow.

At the height of his climax, he called out,

'I don't care if you did kill him. I love you.'

The wind came for them, in the end, as the sun began to sink towards the tops of the reeds, and the air cooled. A tiny breeze, but enough to coast home to the boat-yard. Hot and dry and sticky as they were, they greeted it with regret. As they disentangled their limbs, they looked around at the little plot of grass and wished they could have stayed for ever. It seemed a strange and alien thing to put on their stiff dry clothes. Philippa knew she would remember this tiny place as long as she lived. To be damned together, she thought, was a sort of paradise.

There was barely enough breeze to keep the sail filled; it kept on sagging, then filling again. Barely enough headway to make tiny ripples from the bow, that spread and spread across the enormous mirrored dark width of the Broad as if they would go on to the ends of the earth. Their tremulous calm stayed with them on the whole, slow, wide voyage. There was no need to lean out to balance the boat; or even to change sides as the sail swung over; the boat, a wild thing that morning, was as safe as a child's pram now.

They sat in the stern together, their hands together on the tiller, letting their bodies touch wherever they could.

Their calm even lasted after they saw the police sergeant standing on the edge of the jetty. It was much too late to do anything about anything.

The sergeant stood looking down at them, a creature of power, with that little smile playing about his thin lips. He stood there, rocking gently from his heels to his toes, savouring his moment as they looked up at him.

'You'd better brace yourself for a shock,' he said, and paused. Then he said, with a flick of his hand, 'He's come round.'

Then he went on, like a jury returning a series of verdicts, one after another.

'No fracture of the skull. Irishmen have thick skulls, and so have Krauts. Lucky for you, lad.

'No serious concussion effects. X-ray's normal. They're letting him out of hospital tomorrow. Just keeping an eye on him, for the moment.

'*And* I took the chance to have a word wi' him, before he'd had too much time to think. He admits he started the fight, like you said. And that young tart led him on, out of spite. He's a bit sore at her, but he holds no grudge against you. Said you used to be good mates. He didn't seem too bad a chap at all. For an Irishman. For a Jerry.

'So my Superintendent won't be bringing any charges. I reckon you've got the luck of the devil. But don't let me catch you up to anything else round here. Not even midnight expeditions to haunted mills.'

He let his thin sneering smile break loose then, and took a deep drag of a cigarette he'd been concealing in the cup of his hand, then threw it into the Broad and walked away.

They went on sitting in the dinghy, as dusk fell, and the swallows and house-martins skimmed so low over the water that their bodies touched white sparks from it, in their evening hunt for insects.

'You're *free*,' said Philippa. 'I'm so glad, Brian.'

She did not reach out her hand. They were no longer two of a kind. She no longer had the right.

'Look,' said Brian. 'Didn't they find out you murdered Max?' His eyes dropped, as he lost his courage.

'Brian,' she said. 'I'm sorry to disappoint you, but I didn't murder Max. The Mau Mau did. I only wished him dead. It was the Mau Mau terrorists I killed.

'Two men came to the mission late one night. The house boy, who I never trusted, came and told us they were Mau Mau who had repented, who wanted out. They wanted to be cleansed of their Mau Mau oath, and they knew only Max could do it. They wanted to become Christians.

'I didn't believe a word of it. But Max saw them as brands to be plucked from the burning. He went out to them. He wanted me to come too. But I locked the door behind him, and got down the gun, and watched. He went with them into the house boy's hut and he didn't come out again. Then all three of them came to the door, saying he'd been taken ill, the fools. Such sly voices, evil voices. I shot through the door with the revolver, and kept on shooting. The police said afterwards I missed with the bullets. It was the flying splinters from the door that killed all three.'

'So you're innocent!' said Brian.

Oh, you babe in arms, she thought. What's innocent? But she only said gently,

'I sinned out there from sheer terror, Brian. I sinned with you this afternoon because I wanted to. It makes a difference. Thank you for that, Brian. Thank you for everything.'

His face suddenly looked worried. 'We can go on . . .?'

'Sinning? I'll think about it. I like sinning with you. You're nice to sin with.'

Chapter Fourteen

They sat together in the snack-bar on Peterborough station. Their ways were parting here; he was going north and she was going south. This was . . . a half-way house. They were still full of the sun and the fields, and the evening walks and swims, and the quiet of the churches. They were tanned and relaxed. Brian's nose was peeling with sunburn. But, outside the snack-bar windows, grey-faced, worried-looking people were consulting the tall timetable, looking at their watches and scurrying for their trains.

She could see the changing weather in Brian's face. At times he still smiled at her, the smile that said;

'You're still you, aren't you? Nothing's changed?'

Then he would fall into worried preoccupation, and she knew he was thinking about his parents, in their narrow little council house, living their narrow useful lives. His father was a foreman in a shipyard, and a Freemason. His mother ran whist drives for the church and a National Savings Group, and sang in the Townswomen's Guild Choir. He was wondering how he could explain her to them. Nearly five years older than him, a vicar's daughter, public school, not one of *our* sort. Poor Brian, he was trying to fit the two halves of his life together, like a jigsaw he couldn't get to work.

She knew it was the end. Oh, he would keep his promise;

hitch-hike down to see her, before the end of September. Her parents would make him welcome; Mummy would refer to him as 'Your young friend'.

They would take a kindly interest in him, and blast all his hopes without knowing it. He would never make love to her again, because her father's genuine holiness would flatten him. Or her mother's vision of her daughter as a tragic young widow who would take many years to get over her sad loss.

Brian would wither like a flower. He would despair, as he had to be brought to despair, but she would see he wasn't humiliated. The wound was one he would recover from; he wouldn't be crushed for ever by the fact that she was nearly twenty-five and he was a long way from twenty-one. He would see, in the end, it was the way life went.

He looked up from a flurry of worry that furrowed his brow.

'Are you sure you're not . . . .' He couldn't bring himself to say it, just made a faint gesture at her flat waistline.

'*Quite* sure, Brian.' She couldn't resist a smile of feminine . . . mystique? Superiority? That, too, had come like the opening of a prison door, the prising open of the jaws of a trap. She had found she wasn't pregnant; it was a gift given with the same callous indifference as that policeman's on the jetty. Oh, the ways of the Lord. You threw all His teachings in His face, and He idly threw back blessings.

There must be something wrong with her own inner workings. Max had failed to get her pregnant, and he had tried hard enough. Now Brian had failed too. And so was free of a new trap he had never seen opening at his feet.

She felt a pang of worry about him in the future. He was generous, and there were always traps laid for the feet of the generous, which the mean of spirit saw coming a mile off. She felt she ought to warn him . . . but she couldn't run his future life, any more than he could run hers.

Again she reminded herself that when Brian was a young and vigorous thirty-nine, she would be a cross, wrinkled and menopausal forty-four . . . the traps weren't all on the one side.

'You will write?' asked Brian, anxiously. 'And we can go to Hickling again next year?'

'Yes, Brian,' she said. And thought, but it will be a different, smaller Hickling, and a different Philippa, and a different Brian. If it happens at all.

Meanwhile, thank you, my little Anglo-Saxon warrior, with your sword-arm dedicated to Odin. Thank you, my quite dreadful rule-breaking Father Confessor. The black and holy widow of the martyr can never return. She got broken like a drab in a ditch.

She realised, with a start, that that was really what she had come looking for. Beyond the dream of peace in the greenness, beyond the heat and sweat of the day, beyond the innocent urge to be young and free again, it had lain hidden, wrapped up.

That brought a flurry of conscience. Had she *used* him? She supposed she had. Like she had used the sun and the fields. To rebuild herself; to crawl out of her dead skin, like the larvae of a caddis-fly, into the sun? Searching her conscience, as if before confession, she came to the final conclusion she had. But the sun didn't mind being used; or the fields or the wind. They weren't used *up*; diminished.

She still looked at him with more than a trace of guilt. But he was looking across the snack-bar, to where a long-limbed brown-skinned girl student in very short shorts was bending over her rucksack. There was no thought of being unfaithful on his face but he was interested. As he would be at a beautiful dog or . . . .

She envied the girls who would know him, in the years ahead.

'Brian?' she said.

He came back from a small distance away, and grinned at her.

'Brian,' she said again, suddenly as strict as a mother. 'Brian, some girls get pregnant very easily. Not like me.'

He looked puzzled. 'I don't see that that's going to worry us.'

Sancta simplicitas, she thought, *sancta simplicitas*.

Then she looked at her watch and said 'I think it's time we went. I want to get a seat if I can. It's a long way to Cornwall.'

But she knew Brian would be all right.